THE CENTRE FOR DRAWING: THE FIRST YEAR

Vong Phaophanit   Ansuya Blom   Alexander Roob

The Centre for Drawing:
The First Year
Edited by Angela Kingston
Copy editing by Ian Hunt
Designed by Peter B. Willberg and
Jody Abbott at Clarendon Road Studio
Printed by Clifford Press in Coventry
All photographs are by Nick Manser,
except where indicated
Alexander Roob's drawings were
scanned by Jody Abbott
at Clarendon Road Studio

Published in an edition of 1500,
November 2001

ISBN 0-948327-12-X

Wimbledon School of Art
Merton Hall Road
London SW19 3QA
T +44 (0)20 8408 5000
F +44 (0)20 8408 5050
Art@Wimbledon.ac.uk

The Centre for Drawing has
been generously supported by
the Linbury Trust

Contents

The idea for a centre, devoted to the practice and study of drawing originated in the fine art department at Wimbledon several years ago. The desire to create a focus for drawing stemmed from the high level of attention already given to the subject in the School's courses; from the momentum provided by the work of the Linbury Teaching Fellows in Figurative Drawing, and from the creation of the first masters course in drawing in the UK. The Centre for Drawing, in its present form, developed as a direct result of the appointment of Angela Kingston as Senior Researcher in Drawing, and out of the many discussions that she and I held with students and staff.

The view is often expressed that drawing is so enmeshed into fine art practice, that any attempt to separate it will render it merely academic and neutralise the precise generative capacity that makes it so important. The aspirations of the Centre, however are: firstly, to look at what drawing achieves within the widest possible range of artistic practice; secondly, to examine drawing's enduring significance for all manner of artistic projects; and thirdly, to research the great variety of concepts with which drawing deals. Though the question lying at the heart of the Centre's work is disarmingly simple: how do artists use drawing now?

The phrase 'works on paper' can be a description of far too great a variety of work, including paintings and prints, to serve any useful purpose in defining drawing. Paper is not the only support for drawing, but it is by far the most widespread. Drawings are made with graphite, charcoal, chalk, or ink and with brush and pen. Drawing is flat and monochromatic, and it does not predominantly address colour relationships.

Yet drawing, when understood within this closely defined set of conditions, is seen to accomplish an apparently boundless service for the visual that seems to be in an inverse ratio to its highly bounded material and technical means. There is a creative tension held within this equation, which is substantially undermined when it is claimed that drawing can occur as, rather than in, sculpture, installation, photography, etc. This is to confuse drawing, the thing itself, with the 'drawn', which may be a property or attribute of an image or object. (Spontaneity, immediacy and linearity are examples of attributes that are claimed for drawing.)

The drawn occurs in paintings all the time, but that doesn't make them into drawings. As a painter I experience the interplay between these two modes of working. The relations of drawing, both the act and the object, to other forms of visual production, such as painting, are always changing. There is a great deal to be learned from the attempt to locate these relations much more precisely. John Elderfield begins to do just this when he considers the specific relations between painting and drawing, in the context of Richard Diebenkorn's drawings:

'Drawing... is inherently a process of making equivalence; and the draftsman cannot pretend, as the painter can, that his available means will produce other than abstract equivalents of what he sees. Painting, too, is of course finally a process of equivalence.... In the end, the painter chooses such versions of things as he likes. And how could it be otherwise?... But drawing, unlike painting, picks out the artist's preferences at once. His means are immediately at hand and therefore his meanings are given immediately.... The medium as such can even be ignored, considered purely instrumentally, as an agent of signification like the pen or the pencil in writing and nothing more...'[1]

Artists will always seek to work both within, and against, restrictions imposed by the terrains of genre and medium. For instance Ansuya Blom, the Centre's second resident, made pen drawings directly onto photographic prints. If we want to gain some insight into practices such as this, then a wide frame of reference becomes necessary. The essays that follow demonstrate the extent to which drawing gives rise to as broad a range of interpretative approaches as any other art form.

As explained by Angela Kingston in her essay, artists making drawings are at the heart of the work of the Centre. During a residency they are both the makers of work, and the subjects of debate and critical scrutiny. All three residencies have been very different, but they have all provided the impetus to look at drawings afresh, and to experience the way in which they are able to provoke a sense of wonderment. Robert L.Herbert, writing about Seurat's drawings, describes this perfectly:

'What is a drawing, in the simplest possible terms? Nothing more than a certain arrangement of dark smudges upon a very thin surface made of crushed natural fibers. Hold it up at right angles to the eyes, so that only its thin edge is visible, and all its fragility and insubstantiality becomes apparent; the dark smudges cannot be seen because they lack the thickness to let them appear in relief above the surface; they are contained within the horizontal line facing us. Then suddenly turn the sheet over, face-on. Is it not remarkable how this flat rectangle, darkened here and there, takes on a life of its own?'[2]

I find that the potency of drawing's means remains extraordinary: the precision and speed of the point; the variety of line and trace, and the textures of light and dark; the possibilities of scale given by the page; and the confinement, most often to a single colour. All its possibilities seem bound up in its limitations. This is surely one reason why drawing has at its disposal only what Elderfield calls 'abstract equivalents'. Relieved of other more formal and conclusive tasks, drawing, for successive generations of artists, has remained capable of facilitating unforeseen discovery.

The characteristics of drawing have been with us for a very long time and have been exploited in countless different ways. Despite, or perhaps because of, its longevity, and working now within new technologies and radical art practices, drawing remains instrumental in artistic development. It acts as a record of change and allows us access to the history of the events leading to its conception. Its own complex history and the significance of its contribution to the development of visual culture demands focused study. There is a clear need for a greater understanding of how this most responsive of arts continues to provoke in us a reaction so particular that it remains unshared by other forms of visuality. This is what constitutes the underlying reason for our bringing the Centre for Drawing into being at Wimbledon.

Michael Ginsborg

Michael Ginsborg is an artist and Director of Studies at Wimbledon School of Art.

1 *The Drawings of Richard Diebenkorn*, John Elderfield, The Museum of Modern Art, New York/Houston Fine Art Press, 1988, pp 25–26.

2 *Seurat's Drawings*, Robert L. Herbert, Studio Vista, London, 1965, p 92.

When I was asked to develop the Centre for Drawing at Wimbledon
School of Art (WSA), I questioned whether it should be run like
a typical gallery, which was how it was conceived at the time.
Could not the combined characteristics of drawing and the setting
of an art school better inform the approach we took? Could we do
something both useful for the students and intriguing enough for
the wider art public to venture to Wimbledon? And, in championing
drawing, would we be able to avoid being backward-looking or
worthy?

I wanted, specifically, to respond to the rhythms, characteristics and
priorities of the art school. Instead of importing pre-existing works,
we have set up a studio-gallery, in which works are made *and*
shown. Artists are invited to make drawings during six-week
residencies, one per term. They use the Centre for Drawing as a kind
of retreat – yet, like the students, the artists are under pressure to
come up with something while they are here. After each residency
(and in much the same way that the School transforms itself for
degree shows), there is an exhibition at the Centre that is then open
to the wider public, and this becomes the focus for talks and other
events. Instead of catalogues, we plan to publish a yearly journal,
part of which will document what happens at the Centre (this
publication is its prototype).

Drawing is, of course, vitally important in art education, and it
features as an essential part of the day-to-day practice of most
professional artists. However, from about the mid-eighties to the
later part of the nineties, very little was shown in galleries. The
Centre for Drawing at WSA is part of a surge of activity that is
currently making drawing much more visible. In setting up a gallery
dedicated to drawing (remarkably the UK's first) we are consciously
interfering with its usual status as subsidiary to painting or
sculpture or other art works. By running the Centre for Drawing as
a studio-gallery, we are able to interrogate drawing as both process

and product, giving each equal value. We are also making visible how concerns with process can take precedence over product in the art school and in artists' studios. As a bonus, we are able to look at the practice of exhibiting itself.

Throughout the development of the project Michael Ginsborg, Director of Studies at WSA, has given crucial guidance, particularly with regards to meshing the project with WSA's academic ambitions. As he mentions in the introduction, he and I consulted with groups of staff and students from across the School's specialisms, particularly in order to formulate the wider research questions that we will pose through the Centre over the next few years. Namely: What is drawing's specific capacity to reveal and shape knowledge? What does drawing contribute to new knowledge? Does the act of drawing possess a particular capacity for self-revelation? If so, how does drawing enable the psyche or imagination to manifest itself? How has the artist's sense of drawing been affected by new technologies? Why is drawing still prevalent? How do different societies and groups understand drawing? And why does drawing, in its many different roles and guises, have such widespread cultural importance?

However, having conceived the structure of the Centre for Drawing and the issues it would address, we had doubts. Would artists actually want to come, particularly if they were to be under such intense scrutiny? Would simply offering a bare studio be enough? Would there be enough time in the six weeks to do anything worthwhile – or would this actually be too much time, as drawing very often takes place alongside other activities? And what value would it really have for the students?

We advertised for artists and cast around – and were delighted when Vong Phaophanit showed interest. Phaophanit is internationally known for his sculpture and public art projects, and

1 Erika Naginski, 'Drawing at the
the Crossroads', *Representations*,
no. 92, Fall 2000.

yet it transpired that a 'true' kind of drawing had long been a vitally
important, yet entirely private, facet of his work. He distinguishes
between the diagrams or illustrations he makes for public art works
and drawings which are free of explicit purpose. It was this latter
kind of drawing – which the pressure of his success in recent years
had almost squeezed out of his practice – that the residency would
allow him to rediscover. Having previously – as he said in a
conversation with Guy Brett which appears in this publication –
been 'very protective of this quiet activity', he would go public with
it for the first time at the Centre for Drawing. Yet Phaophanit was
apprehensive: it had been such a long time since he had found any
real space to do this kind of drawing that he could not envisage
what he might do.

Phaophanit worked quietly and with concentration, responding to
the emptiness of the room and its echo and the sounds from outside.
As he said to Brett 'I was almost transforming myself into a sponge,
absorbing everything that surrounded me.... And then I would
squeeze that sponge and a drawing would happen on that blank
paper.' Here, in these drawings, Phaophanit achieved both
sensuality and 'in-betweeness', a quality Claire Oboussier discusses,
citing his description of his working process 'as being between the
conscious and the unconscious, between the intuitive and the
intentional, as floating between control and the uncontrollable'.

Erika Naginski, who contributes an afterword to this book, has
previously written about the extraordinary capacity drawn and
calligraphic marks have to translate rapidly from one function to
another.[1] Discussing drawing's fugitive properties, she asserts:
'there is no fixed and absolute identity – aesthetic, semiotic, or
otherwise – that we can attribute to the trace.' Naginski then goes
on to describe how drawing is nevertheless claimable by the artist,
referring to 'drawing's behaviour, procedures, and aims [being]
configured, altered, manipulated, disrupted, and eventually

affirmed by its capricious ability to translate the inside world to the outside world and back again.' Reading this, I began to think of Phaophanit's drawings in part as escapology (understandably he resents his work being closed down by easy references to his South East Asian background) and also, paradoxically, as centring. Constantly shifting away from any simple identification, his drawings include an extraordinary range of marks to which we attribute differing temperaments and associations: there are calligraphic notations, exuberant squiggles and doodles, languid and dirty marks and prettily showy spots, for example. The rapid shifts between styles and approaches in these drawings, and their urgent personal expression, combine to bear out Naginski's assertions that while we cannot attach definitive significance to drawn marks, they can be uncannily precise in what they communicate.

It follows that Phaophanit was visibly happy during his six weeks of drawing. We had thought, to begin with, that Phaophanit might make preparatory drawings for future sculptures while he was with us. Instead, he worked with deliberate purposelessness. He made an astonishing number of works (about ninety), especially when you consider that his typical output is one or two sculptures a year. Mostly using brush and ink, and occasionally pencil, Phaophanit worked on seven sketch-books simultaneously, each of them following a particular strand of ideas; loose-leaf drawings proliferated outwards from these books and were laid in rows on the floor. He seemed to become like some of the students here who use drawing to house an excess of possibility.

From my own perspective as a curator, the Centre for Drawing is exhilarating as way of working, the whole process accelerated to fit into just a few weeks. A few days after Vong Phaophanit arrived, I was asking him if he had an image we could use for the invitation card. Drawings were no sooner made than selected for framing. Then we were immediately into the exhibition, intense public discussion with the artist and a programme of related lectures. (Compare this to anything up to about three to five years' incubation for many exhibitions on the part of the curator, and perhaps even longer for the artist.)

By contrast to the experimental nature of some aspects of the project, I approached the nuts-and-bolts of the exhibition in a very usual manner; we had a preview, typical signage and information, a visitor's book, and so on, and this has continued, more or less, for the second two residency exhibitions this year. If I am doing anything different it is to hang back slightly from the artists, hoping that students will benefit from many of the spontaneous exchanges that a curator usually enjoys.

Ansuya Blom was the second artist-in-residence in the spring of 2001. Drawing is, by contrast to Phaophanit, both central and constant within her practice, and visible in large-scale works on canvas, in sculptures, and even in one of her films. And, while Phaophanit might be seen as laying hold of an otherwise overwhelming surge of ideas, Blom's drawings seem charged with circumspection.

Used to an intensely private working environment, Blom came to the Centre for Drawing as a way of putting herself to the test and in order to seek out a number of breakthroughs. She wanted to speed up her drawing, to see what this might produce, and there was also a hope in the air that she did not quite want to verbalise. Knowing that she would need to come prepared, she brought with her ink-jet prints of photographs of a stark corridor and white gouache pens to make drawings onto the photographic images.

Sometimes the white lines on the resulting drawings survey the corridor like spider's gossamer, especially those first threads that cast out across an empty space. At other times, it is as if the massing

2 The statements, in order of appearance, are by Rod Bugg, artist and Principal of WSA, David Maclagan, an artist and art therapist who was visiting the School, Bob Mason, Course Leader, MA Fine Art: Drawing, and Anne Adamson, MA Fine Art: Drawing student.

3 For the record, she made approximately twelve gouache pen on ink-jet photographic print drawings and eight smaller works.

4 WSA and Tate conference 'Contemporary Drawing: from the Doodle to the Digit', 2 March 2001, Tate Britain, London.

white lines have seeped in like ectoplasm. In some of the pictures, there are drawings of chairs, tables and clothes amongst the entanglement of lines.

Talks by tutors and students took place each day of her exhibition, and one commentator spoke of her drawings as being evidence of 'a process of withdrawing, of intuition, of touch, of tactile engagement of the inquiring hand across the page'; he also responded to the 'different speeds of mark' and the 'quality of movement and menace'. Another said he thought 'of things coming unravelled, of fragile webs connecting a chilling institutional space'. And a third was reminded of sculptures by Eva Hesse, with their 'combination of minimal, monochromatic materials with gesture' and their 'jokey, sinister, absurd and slightly uneasy' qualities.

There was considerable discussion about an otherworldly feel to Blom's WSA drawings. One student talked about a property of the line: 'It stays the same, it doesn't go with the perspective ... it seems to belong to another dimension.'[2] I would suggest that this quality relates to the quiet breakthrough Blom wanted. Over the years, her drawings have often alluded to the body as a mass of fragile flesh, and recently something more ghostly has been intimated. Here, pushing herself to work at greater speed,[3] her drawings have managed to harness this strange, out-of-body, ethereal energy.

Pared down and, thanks to the pen she used, instantly permanent, Blom's line swoops, veers and wavers. I recently heard Bernard Burgoyne, a psychoanalyst, talking about drawing and writing – practices he regards as being inseparably founded in struggle. He argued that two fundamental, yet conflicting, imperatives are represented in drawing and writing through marks that venture out into the unknown like arrows and marks that form safe enclosures.[4] Blom seems to put these opposites into play: a darting straight line is seen to stumble, a self-protecting curve to leap across the page.

She subverts, therefore, the very function of the line. In putting the line into play in this way, she makes me think of how, daily and almost imperceptibly, we are paradoxical and playful in our attempts to cope with the pull of contradictory desires in our lives.

Ian Hunt pursues some expansive descriptions and interpretations of Blom's drawings in his essay. A rich discussion between Michael Ginsborg and the artist is recorded too, in which Blom is concerned to keep the meaning and purpose of these works open. A phrase of hers which emerged early in her residency, about her interest in 'the lines that go out from drawing', resonates here. For Blom, drawing is an activity which is essentially unbounded, and, as Hunt develops in his essay, free.

Alexander Roob was the third resident at the Centre for Drawing. He has a highly specific drawing practice – a drawing method, even – in which he makes sequences of observational drawings in diverse locations that attract his interest. He has previously drawn, for example, at the United Nations, in an operating theatre and in a sausage factory, and he came to WSA because he was attracted to the idea of making drawings in the School's theatre department. He also wanted to make a portrait of the everyday life of an art school: it seemed logical after drawing in art museums and, for a brief time, in his own studio, to go to another kind of place associated with art. So, whereas Phaophanit sought to break from certain demands and Blom was in pursuit of change, Roob's residency was entirely consistent with his usual way of working.

He was seen around the School making his linear pencil drawings on A5 sheets of paper. He likes to work quickly, entering what one commentator has called 'a state of gliding, unfocused, attentive-ness'.[5] The Centre for Drawing was used to lay out and edit the 482 drawings he produced into sequences, a much slower and more conscious process through which visual narratives emerge. For his exhibition, he displayed about a quarter of these drawings as strands of story, that could be 'read' from right to left as well as from left to right, in rows on narrow tables.

Roob responded favourably when I suggested that his drawing is anti-pedagogic: 'I like the term. I think by contrast to the former artists-in-residence I insist on drawing as an autonomous medium with its own advantages and limitations, and not a basic pedagogic subject that prepares for other media.' Neither does he use it in an introspective way. 'I am a reporter,' he says.

Roob worked for long stretches in the life room, where students make drawings and sculptures of the naked model. In this setting, as Eric Ziegeweid discusses in his essay, and as explored in Roob's conversation with Kate Macfarlane, the artist's strict drawing method gave rise to particularly curious effects. Confusions emerge between a model drawn in outline and the students' drawings of the same model reproduced in the same outline on the same page. A naked, anguished man with hands covering his face, who is being casually ignored by the students at his side, is discovered to be not a 'real' man, but an inert form made of plaster.

To me, this absence of differentiation in Roob's method of depiction suggests, at times, a lack of concern for human flesh and experience. At other times, I perceive Roob's drawings as congenial note-takings of the often curious activities with which we fill our lives to give them meaning. At Wimbledon his drawing method served, in particular, to lay bare our shared compunction to register our temporary presence in the world. How many faces will be drawn, how many bodies will be sculpted, before we are satisfied? As such, Roob's spare line here is pure pathos. Roob himself noticed, in particular, 'a slow shifting from a generalising, marionette-like view of the figure towards a more individualistic and bodily sensibility.'

Alexander Roob's exhibition at the Centre for Drawing was during the students' degree shows. I enjoyed going from one to the other, moving from Roob's drawings of theatre students making their final presentation pieces, to seeing these same works finished and on display. Roob had documented the transitory moments of living and being and making at the School, catching hold of the now invisible industry of it all – and rendering this in outline, a form of drawing that is, by coincidence, particularly associated with process (in, for instance, the use of architectural drawings to plan the future construction of buildings) and transience (in, for example, cartoons or sequential diagrams).

Phase two of the Centre for Drawing will be the development of facilities for a study collection of drawings, to include examples from each of the residencies. We plan also to revisit drawing residents' practices over several years, to examine the long-term effects of their engagement with drawing at WSA. And we will involve people from other disciplines in future residencies so as to compare how drawing – with its capacity to communicate, its provisional, speedy nature, its function as visual thinking – is used elsewhere, in order to address our question about drawing's 'widespread cultural importance'. Having the theatre courses at WSA means that we are well placed to invite scenographers or choreographers to the Centre, for example.

Most importantly, the driving force in our explorations will continue to be the contemporary character of drawing as a process. Influenced in this way, the Centre for Drawing is a practice-led gallery which finds a natural home in the art school.

Angela Kingston

Angela Kingston is a curator and writer, and Senior Researcher in Drawing at Wimbledon School of Art.

Vong Phaophanit lives and works in London. He was born in 1961 in Savannakhet, Laos, and from 1980 to 1985 he studied at the École des Beaux Arts, Aix-en-Provence, France. He held a Deutscher Akademischer Austauschdienst Berliner Künstlerprogramm (DAAD) Scholarship from 1996 to 1997.

Vong Phaophanit's solo exhibitions include *tok tem dean kep kin bo dai (what falls to the ground but can't be eaten)*, Chisenhale Gallery, London, and Ikon Gallery, Birmingham (1991); *neon rice field*, Serpentine Gallery, London, and Tate Gallery, London, as part of the Turner Prize exhibition (1993), and *atopia*, DAAD, Berlin (1997), and Royal Festival Hall, London (1998). Since 1990, he has shown in group exhibitions in major international museums and galleries, including the Museo Nacional Centro de Arte Reina Sofía, Madrid (1994), The Irish Museum of Modern Art, Dublin (1995), De Appel, Amsterdam (1995), the National Gallery of Contemporary Art, Sydney (1997), and Galerie für Zeitgenössiche Kunst, Leipzig, Germany (2001). His work was included in the Aperto at the Venice Biennale in 1993, and in the 1997 Johannesburg Biennale. Vong Phaophanit made his drawings public for the first time with his exhibition at the Centre for Drawing at WSA in December 2000.

Vong Phaophanit has also realised several public art projects, including *ash and silk wall*, Greenwich Thames Barrier Park, London, commissioned by Public Art Development Trust for Greenwich Borough Council (1993), and *sky lines*, Tyrebagger, Aberdeen, commissioned by Art in Partnership for the Tyrebagger Trust (2001).

Vong Phaophanit is represented by Stephen Friedman Gallery, London.

I see this residency as a point of
departure for a rediscovery of a
dimension of my work that has been
marginalized by the demands of
large-scale three-dimensional works.
Although I have never stopped
drawing in my practice the nature
and function of drawing has changed:
it has often been confined to the
role of communication of technical
information or illustration of
proposed art works. I wish to return
to drawing as the most basic of acts –
linked directly to the body and
without a specific function. The
residency offers me a chance to work
with complete openness with,
simultaneously, the benefits of an
unfamiliar defined space and
duration.

Vong Phaophanit, October 2000

Vong Phaophanit at work at the
Centre for Drawing, November 2000

neon rice field
rice and clear red neon tubes 1993
1500×450 cm
Tate Gallery, Millbank, London
photo: Tate Gallery
courtesy of the Weltkunst Foundation

from light, 1800×600 cm,
blue neon Laotian script and
34 minute, 250×400 cm video
projection, 1995
Angel Row Gallery, Nottingham
photo: Gary Kirkham

woodworm, bamboo,
polybutadiene rubber and
zinc-coated steel plates
53×396 cm, 1999
Stephen Friedman Gallery, London
photo: Stephen White
courtesy of the artist and Stephen
Friedman Gallery, London

sky lines
drilled tree trunks
2001
Tyrebagger, Aberdeen
photo: Mike Davidson
commissioned by Art in Partnership
for the Tyrebagger Trust

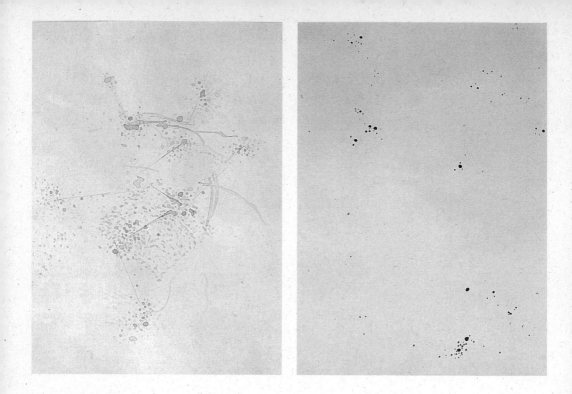

mute
ink and wash on paper
41.5×29 cm
2000
photo: Rosie Potter

not born
ink and wash on paper
triptych, each part 41.5×29 cm
2000

as a raven, ink and wash on paper, 41.5×29 cm, 2000

yesterday, ink and wash on paper, 41.5×29 cm, 2000

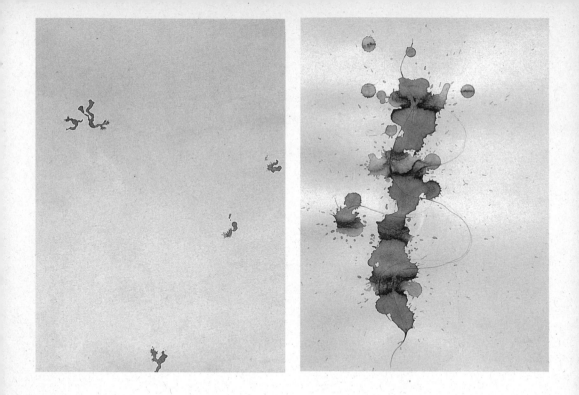

sotto
ink and wash on paper
41.5×29 cm
2000

a silk purse
ink and wash with pencil on paper
41.5×29 cm
2000
private collection

as a fish
ink and wash on paper
41.5×29 cm
2000

hoarse
ink and wash on paper
41.5×29 cm
2000

voce
ink and wash on paper
41.5×29 cm
2000

a sow's ear
ink and wash on paper
41.5×29 cm
2000

Sketchbook pages
ink and wash on paper
29.5 × 29.5cm
2000

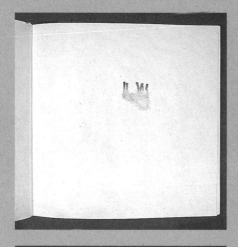

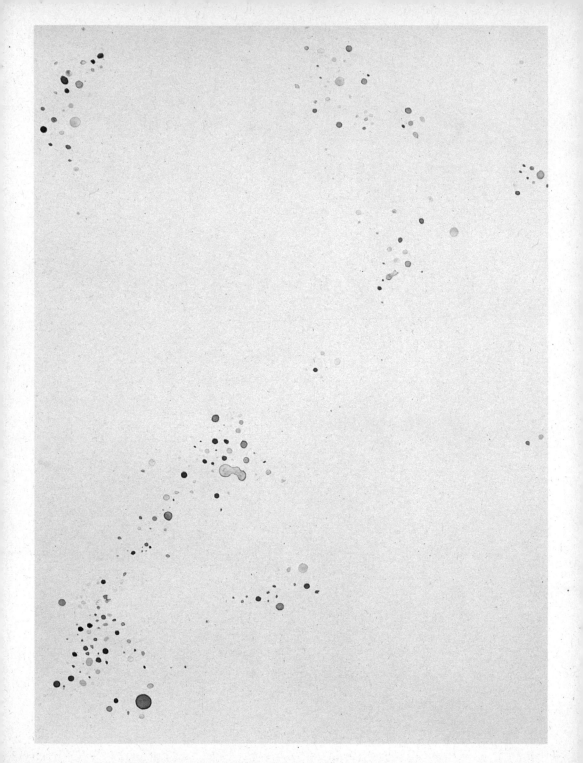

Two-part untitled drawing, watercolour on paper, each 41.5×29 cm, 2000

Vong Phaophanit's exhibition at the Centre for Drawing, December 2000

Vong Phaophanit:

Since I've been practising in this country for almost fifteen years now, I have come across Guy's name several times, but never had the chance really to converse with him. It was always in my mind, my wish, that one day I would find the opportunity, but I never expected that it would be in front of an audience! I just have to take it as it is now, there's no way of backing out. And also I never expected that the conversation would centre around, or on, or about, drawings. Especially because I have, up to now, been very protective of these quiet activities. At the same time I know very well how important these activities are amongst other projects that I am doing, or have done in the past. Up to now, discussions on drawing have been some kind of missed opportunity because we always talk about aspects of drawing that I don't always find very interesting.... Previous drawings of mine are mainly illustrative or technical. Although they are, it's true, part of the richness of drawing, I always thought of them as secondary in terms of challenge and in the questions that they may propose to an artist. Then, just a year ago, I met Angela at a private view, and she told me about the work she was doing here, and mentioned the residency. I think you asked me, Angela, if I was doing drawings, and I just said 'yes' but it was almost like 'let's talk about something else'. We didn't have a chance to talk again about the residency for almost a year until one day Angela asked me if I would like to do it. Suddenly I felt the pressure to fit in with the idea of drawing, and I've always found excuses to avoid that challenge, by digging up other types of challenges. That's why I accepted it, knowing it would be a very concentrated time. I felt it was the right moment.

Guy Brett:

Well, Vong, I'm also very happy to have this opportunity to talk with you. There are a number of things I would like to ask you about your drawings, and some comments I would like to make in response to them. You used the phrase just now, 'the richness of drawing'. You said that the kind of drawing you had been doing in the past was technical drawing, connected with realising your works, and you said that perhaps the existence of these practical drawings is an aspect of the richness of drawing. The richness of the role of drawing is certainly one of the most fascinating things about it. As well as 'rich' I would like to use the word 'persistent'. Drawing has never been outmoded. It is something you can trace through the whole history of art, from the caves to computers. And, broader than this, drawing is something that runs through the whole of culture. It was Derek Boshier who pointed out to me once that a drawing lies behind virtually every manufactured object in our environment. Before there was a lampshade, a window-catch, a pair of shoes, there was a drawing. That's the persistence of drawing in one sense, but obviously here what I would like to concentrate on are the drawings which have come out of your residency. One thing that you said when we were talking yesterday evening, which intrigued me a lot, was that you said that it was not so much the process of making the mark which was important in these drawings, or applying the brush to the paper, but the act of taking the brush away from the paper. That seems to me fascinating, and it also ties in with the obviously very important role that the empty space, the empty piece of paper plays in your drawings.

The drawings in the exhibition all have a common starting-point. They are all results of an experience of the unconscious within this given space: the empty page. They are also moments of vacillation between consciousness and unconsciousness. All these moments have to be in harmony, of the same intensity. For me there is no hierarchy of importance. That's why I found it very difficult to start a drawing. On one hand, you want to be fully prepared, fully in control; at the same time your emotion, your energy somehow tends to dictate something else. You are constantly moving or feeling one or the other, all the time. That's what I wanted to find in drawing. When I was doing the technical drawings, it was different. The

purpose was different; it served a purpose somehow. Here, the result doesn't serve a purpose. Except, perhaps, for creating a new way of seeing, of thinking.

You say that it's difficult to begin, to know how to begin. Is it also difficult to know how to stop, to end?

To end is even more difficult. Somehow to start you have to jump in. But how do you leave it? Do you leave the space by smashing the door, or by rubbing out your traces, your footprints, or by clinging on the edge. There are so many possible ways of dealing with that.

Do you have any thoughts about the relationship – you used the word 'trace' in passing just now – about the relationship, or the contradiction, between the trace and the sign? I've always thought this was a fascinating problematic in twentieth-century art. There have been occasional attempts by artists to simply catch a trace of some pre-existing energy or force. Sometimes almost Dadaistic acts, or absurd acts. For example, Yves Klein putting a wet canvas on the top of his car and driving from Paris to Nice at full speed in order to try to catch traces of the wind currents on the canvas, and then exhibiting the canvas in an exhibition. Presumably this would be a trace rather than a sign. But on the other hand, these two worlds, these two categories, often seem very intimately related to one another: traces can become signs, and signs can become traces. In the Chinese tradition, in painting and calligraphy, there is clearly a connection between those two ambiguous entities. The artists try to create in themselves the state of being receptive to energies that may flow through them and come out onto the piece of paper or silk, which is, again, both a trace and a sign. I see a similar process going on in your drawings.

Yes. What I have tried to do is to increase that ambiguity between the trace and the sign. I would never feel what it is to

be in one camp rather than the other. And that's how
I always feel in my life too, the way I perceive reality, the
way I use language, the way I eat food, as well....

How does it come out in that way?

> When we talk about all these notions of traces
> and signs, there is something that I am always
> suspicious about, the notion of purity. I don't
> believe in purity, whether it is used in religion, or
> politics, or even in art... I would never join that
> discourse. I prefer to retain my position in
> between. The notion of purity has often been
> badly interpreted, used in a negative way, to
> divide... I'm always suspicious of this.

Oh yes, I myself am thinking of a notion of impurity. Another aspect of the
sign-trace dichotomy is the extension of the notion of the sign to include
script and writing, and notation systems of all kinds. I think we find this
richness in, for example, Paul Klee: the conjunction between script, even if
his are invented scripts, and various sorts of notation systems like musical
notation, or botanical illustration, or meteorological mapping, or lines of
force, all fusing together. This came to my mind knowing that you have
made works based on script in the past, the Laotian script.

> The Laotian script was used for various reasons. The most
> obvious one is the visual effect. But, you know, I never give any
> translation of the words in these works, and this is really to
> create a sense of frustration in the viewer. The average viewer
> doesn't have any access to the semantic meanings, and
> somehow feels like an outsider. This work goes back ten years,
> to a time when I felt it was a way of raising all the issues about
> identity and culture. That was in the early nineties when the
> black and Asian movement was very fertile and very active.

You felt strongly connected with that?

> I wasn't directly connected. Their actions couldn't include someone like me because I was coming from somewhere else. They were born in this country so they were dealing with different issues.

Going back to your drawings and the experience of your exhibition. When I first walked in I saw the similarities in all the drawings. But after a few minutes I became aware that each drawing took on a very different identity, a very different character, an individual character that I found intriguing. Actually, I used a rather fanciful analogy, and said that it reminded me of the songs of different birds, and then you said that actually sound had been an important element in the background of these drawings. That hadn't occurred to me at all. It's extremely interesting. Perhaps you could say something about that.

> Yes. The way we selected for the show was deliberately to maintain the individuality and character of each drawing. We tried to keep them as separate as possible. Each of them contains its own hidden world. But the sound itself... well, when I first arrived in that room it was completely empty. It took me a while to find a place to sit down almost. The sound in that room was a tremendous echo. Behind it is the sculpture courtyard, so there's always something happening there. And further down there's a primary school, where every two hours or so the children would come out to play. I think the sound managed to get inside this room and the way I was preparing myself for the drawing sessions – I was, as you mentioned, almost transforming myself into a sponge, absorbing everything that surrounded me. And then I would squeeze that sponge, and a drawing would happen on that blank paper. That's a very simplified version of how these works were

produced. I limited myself to one or two tools to make these drawings, mainly brushes and a very small amount of pencil. But somehow with the brush you can create different sounds, different tonalities. I'm not talking about music, just sound. The actual process is very quiet. You just dip your brush in the water, you rinse the brush, you're not thinking about what a sculptor would do, cutting, banging or melting. It's a very quiet, an extremely quiet activity, but at the same time, through that silence, somehow sounds reappear and that's why I talk about sound. And again once when the show was up and I was on my own in the room I could almost hear the noise come out of those drawings, that's how I felt. Not necessarily a living creature, but all this sound, scratching or pushing or rubbing or...

Yes, that brings my mind back to the interchangeability between the different art forms and between the graphic, let's say, and other forms of energy. Sound is obviously a form of energy, as well. To get a bit more general again about drawing... I very much wanted, myself, when I was putting together the exhibition 'Force Fields: Phases of the Kinetic', to include drawings beside the kinetic machines. You might, for example, have a tiny drawing by Wols and a little further away a wild machine of Tinguely. I wanted to consider all these works as an artist's creation of force fields, or energy fields. I wanted to suggest that artists also, like scientists, create models of the universe and even if the artist is dabbling with a piece of paper, it is as much a map of reality, of the whole of reality including oneself. It's the artist's model, a poetic investigation into the nature of the cosmos. I think in the face of the cosmos it must necessarily be modest. Wols himself said that all we can do is 'tell our little earthbound tales on little bits of paper'. I felt, Vong, there is something of a link between your drawing process and scientific investigation. I know it sounds fanciful to say it. But I think that you are, through the medium of the brush and the water, finding evidence of a kind of self-generation of forms or energies or entities. One could link that with what you said about these works having no purpose, but that spirit of having no purpose is perhaps a way of producing something which actually is linked very intimately with a dimension much larger than oneself.

I perfectly agree with what you just said – it was an investigation. The way I felt during the residency was almost like a blind person, not knowing his path, but knocking left and right with his stick. I mean, each drawing gave me some kind of false fulfilment. It gave me confidence to start again, but at the same time each time it was with hesitation, I had to stop and consider. It's that fight, that marriage between hesitation and control...

By an extraordinary coincidence, this afternoon before I came here, I was leafing through a book I have called *The Scientific Image*, and there was a rather fascinating experiment carried out by an American zoologist, Asa Schaefer, in 1920. The experiment consisted of asking a blindfolded person to walk in a straight line, and this person set off walking what they thought was a straight line. But it turned out to be a large spiral. The person went round and round in an ever-diminishing and rather beautiful ellipse which happened to end when they tripped up over a tree trunk!

Sounds like a terrible story about my residency!

Question from the audience:
I would like to ask Vong what he feels he has gained from this residency?

It really reinforced the value of that activity. I feel almost re-energized by the whole experience. And it will probably have a direct effect on future work that will come. But there are things that I would not be able to translate, to replace what I've done with

drawing. They have their own different languages. One cannot be replaced with another one. But one can kind of inject.

You've described a very contemplative process that you've gone through. How will all that affect the main core of the work that you have been doing? How will it alter it, or indeed inspire it?

I have no ideas so far, because it is too fresh. I hope it will make me more demanding of future projects. That's all I can tell you at this stage.

Do you find your drawings precious?

The time I spent doing them, yes, was precious. They are what they are…. The main thing is the experience. Through that experience things did take place, you know, and came to the surface, but now somehow they've been exorcised.

What I meant was: precious in the sense you would want to keep them.

No, I never want to keep my work.

That reminds me that another mode of drawing is the ephemeral and performative. I can remember some rather fascinating performative drawing, the production of drawings in a theatricalized way very different to Vong's approach. I once took part in a rather amazing drawing experience by an artist called Laure Chenard, which took place in Rotterdam. She was one of the artists participating in a performance festival. She occupied a room and the door was locked. There was always a queue of people waiting outside and you went in one at a time. We didn't know what to expect and the people coming out had been asked by the artist not to tell us, or they didn't feel like telling us. What actually happened was you got inside this enormous baggy sweater with Laure

Chenard and she did a drawing of you by touch in the dark inside this sweater. I still have my drawing somewhere.... Her notion was that she couldn't think of people in the mass, she couldn't think of people in terms of groups, she could only think of the individual and this was her way of making work with an individual – there was no audience. It was a very constructed, theatricalized, but intimate experience. I don't know how other people reacted. I was typically English and reserved....

Vong, you spoke of the particular environment of the exhibition room, empty and echoing. And outside there was activity that you spoke of as sound, but you said that the sound was not music, that you didn't relate to the sounds in the way you relate to music. Music is connected. All the marks that you make look connected, or are they disconnected? In your mind are they separated, disconnected?

Yes, they are disconnected and that is precisely what I wanted to do, to keep these marks at their primary stage without any safety net, without references.

Guy Brett has written extensively for the art press since the 1960s and has also organised exhibitions. His most recent exhibitions, for which he also wrote catalogue essays, have been 'Force Fields: Phases of the Kinetic' (MACBA, Barcelona and Hayward Gallery, London, 2000) and 'Li Yuan-chia' (Camden Arts Centre and touring, 2001). His books include *Through Our Own Eyes: Popular Art and Modern History* (New Society, Philadelphia, 1986), *Transcontinental: Nine Latin American Artists* (Verso, London and New York, 1990), and *Exploding Galaxies: The Art of David Medalla* (Kala Press, London, 1995).

Looking at these drawings, pondering what is sayable about them,
I am reminded of a little-known piece by Vong Phaophanit
commissioned in 1995 and entitled *From Light* which includes a
circular piece of film without beginning or end. The film has been
shot and edited so as to render it equivocal – its informational level
is suspended: is it a seascape or a desertscape? Swept by rain or
sand? Is its occasional yellow hue due to fading sunlight, an
industrial smog, a post-nuclear cloud or simply a technical ruse?
This piece manages somehow to be replete with resonance, with
atmosphere, and yet simultaneously impossible to locate or identify.
What also becomes evident, as the film circulates, is that there is
no eye controlling the camera – it tracks the movements of a body
and its (the camera's) own eye is left to play at will, its auto-focus
desperately grasping at surfaces upon which it might fix, only to
blur again as it moves on. It is the oneiric, other-worldly quality
of this piece where reference points become abstracted and tease
our efforts to restrain meaning which was recalled by these new
drawings.

Reference has always been an important dimension of Vong
Phaophanit's practice. It has been approached and challenged
in various ways – ironically, wittily, teasingly and occasionally
politically. The artist has often achieved this by discreetly
subverting the narratives attached to the materials he uses,
reasserting their very materiality and creating new fusions of
substances. This play of metaphor, material and cultural reference,
the particular alchemy of these elements as they lived and breathed
in the works, could lead on occasions to a kind of silence, a
suspension of chatter, where generation of meaning becomes
possible. It is as if the residency at Wimbledon freed Phaophanit to
make an excursus further into this dimension of his practice. The
return to drawing (and it was a return, as drawing had been
Phaophanit's formative and fundamental art practice) allowed
a more direct, visceral approach to this process of transfusion.

The paradox of directness and mediation in the making of art has been exquisitely explored in the terms of his previous work, where cultural encoding is always brought into a living, organic relationship with sensuous production, creating a kind of in-betweeness. Guy Brett, in conversation with Phaophanit, was receptive to this duality or paradox in the drawings; he speaks of a historical contradiction between the trace and the sign – the trace being an energy or force directly captured and the sign being a cipher that is culturally mediated. He suggests ways in which these two apparently polarised fields might possibly come to coalesce (as in the Chinese tradition of calligraphy for example) and sees this kind of embodiment taking place in Phaophanit's drawings. Phaophanit responds to this suggestion in the following way: 'Yes, what I've tried to do is to increase that ambiguity between the trace and the sign. I would never feel what it is to be in one camp rather than the other. And that's how I always feel in my life too, the way I perceive reality, the way I use language.' The drawings seem to be an inti-mate exploration of this cross-fertilisation of signifying fields. He goes on to explain to Guy Brett: 'there is something that I'm always suspicious about, the notion of purity. I don't believe in purity, whether it is used in religion, or politics or even in art... I would never join that discourse. I prefer to retain my position in between.'

Phaophanit's practice has always been articulated in this interstitial space. In a recent conversation he spoke to me of how he addressed this in his approach to the drawings. 'I found it very difficult to start a drawing. On one hand, you want to be fully prepared, fully in control [but] at the same time your emotion, your energy somehow tends to dictate something else.' He describes a kind of ritual where in the mornings, for two hours, he would try to 'evacuate the other works' (previous and other current works). It was through the dot series that he was able to do this – he describes this series as being between the conscious and the unconscious, between the intuitive

and the intentional, as floating between control and the uncontrollable. At first he worked with drops of pure water which he then returned to and 'injected' colour into. He explained that this 'exercise brought me closer to drawing' and that finally it came to have a visual significance of its own. Then in the afternoons he started to draw 'and then it was very free – I let forms come – sometimes hard, dry forms and at other times fluid, mercurial forms... sometimes very fast, like I was throwing them out.' Some of these drawings were left in that first state. Others he returned to and reworked – but not in order to perfect or finish them but rather to 'efface the traces', traces that is of reference, of structure, of 'attachment'. This was a process of perpetually enlarging the space of the drawing itself, of eliding narratives and forms that could attenuate that space, a process of distancing definition. And then what also became vital to the drawing process was how to stop, when to, as Phaophanit puts it 'lever les mains' (raise your hands). Sometimes he made this exit by effacing or diluting, at other times he marked it strongly on the page.

It is not that Phaophanit is insisting that the drawings be free of reference but rather that they cannot refer to any pre-existing narratives. They must arrive at the point where they can exist on their own terms, in their own idiom. The chosen method of titling the drawings is an extension of this. Set phrases, metaphors, figures of speech have been disseminated, scattered into meaningless fragments and then simply assigned to the drawing with which they seemed to have some physical affinity.

This opening up of reference and of meaning is poignantly addressed through the 'empty gesture' series of drawings. Rendered in white pigment, human figures float like blanched shadows on the page, engaged in some activity but with the object of that activity effaced. Their gestures have become functionless, without cultural reason. That to which we would normally turn to establish the meaning of the image, to enable us to ground it and to identify it in some way, has been lifted out, leaving us momentarily tantalised and then curiously calmed. As viewers, we are strangely liberated by this lack of anecdotal information. The gesture itself would somehow have been much less allusive, much less accessible to the imaginary, had its object been present. The white used in this series of 'invisible drawings' literally challenges our act of looking – we have to move and shift continually so that the light catches the surface of the dried pigment and creates a reflection that renders the image visible. Phaophanit describes the way he worked on this series: 'You have to move fast – if the ink dries you can no longer see what you are drawing and you can never see the whole picture while you work. You are in a constant state of doubt, of risk.' It is for this reason that the figurative was chosen uniquely for this series. An abstract form would not have presented the same challenge or engendered the same risk. Here the image was fleeing before his eyes as he worked on it – 'It was like losing your sight while working, like walking in a fog – you can't see in front or behind, just where you are at that moment.'

The drawings Phaophanit produced during his time in residence at the Centre for Drawing are offerings in the sense that Bataille has written about. Bataille explored the realm of the gift, and others after him such as Cixous have expanded these ideas through the

French notion of *dépense*, with its playful duality of meaning. Expressing both expenditure without thought of return and, literally, the undoing of thought, *dépense* embraces those dimensions of human culture that are irreducible to the orthodox dyad of production and consumption. Phaophanit's new drawings emerge from an economy such as this; one of risk, of giving wherein there has been a relinquishment of the constraints of conscious thought. They issue from a working process which has dispensed with the safety net.

Claire Oboussier

Claire Oboussier is a writer and artist. Her doctoral thesis was on the work of Roland Barthes and Hélène Cixous (Bristol, 1994). She has published essays on the work of both these authors as well as on poetic synaesthesia. She has written about Vong Phaophanit's work for the past sixteen years and collaborated with him on numerous projects. She has recently produced a book with him on a year spent in Berlin for the DAAD scholarship. Currently she is working on three commissioned works in collaboration with Phaophanit.

All quotations are from a recent unpublished conversation between the artist and the author unless otherwise indicated in the text.

Ansuya Blom was born in 1956 in Groningen, the Netherlands, and studied at Koninklijke Akademie, The Hague (1973–74) and at Ateliers '63, Haarlem (1974–76). From 1980 to 1981 she was in residence at PS1 in New York. Since 1976 she has lived and worked in Amsterdam.

Ansuya Blom has had one-person exhibitions at the Stedelijk Museum, Amsterdam (1990), Sala Montcada de la Fundació Barcelona,'la Caixa' (1994), Ikon Gallery, Birmingham (1994), Douglas Hyde Gallery, Dublin (1995), Camden Arts Centre, London (1995), CCA, Glasgow (1995), and the Stedelijk Museum, Schiedam, the Netherlands (1999). She has also exhibited extensively in group exhibitions, including at The Drawing Center, New York (1993). She represented The Netherlands at the 1985 São Paulo Biennale and exhibited in the Aperto at the 1990 Venice Biennale.

The artist has had one-person screenings of her films at the Museum of Modern Art, New York, and at the Institute of Contemporary Art, Philadelphia (both 1999). Her films have been broadcast on Kunstkanaal (1990) and on VPRO tv (1996). They have also featured in national and international film festivals in New York (1987), Toronto (1987), Knokke (1995), Utrecht (1990, 1996) and Rotterdam (1988, 1990, 1993, 1996, 1998).

Ansuya Blom teaches at the Rijksakademie in Amsterdam and is represented by Galerie Van Gelder, Amsterdam.

One thing I am interested in is the link
between writing and drawing, with
drawing deriving a sense of indirect
narrative, linguistic potency and
freedom because of this link. I am
interested, too, in the lines that go out
from drawing – not only to writing,
but also to film-making and other areas
of work.

Ansuya Blom, January 2001

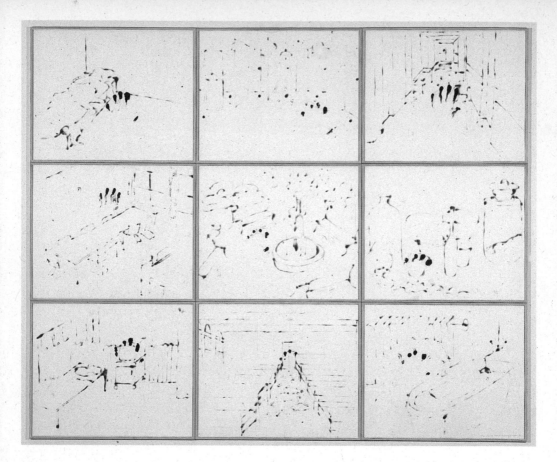

The mute house I
printing ink on burnt paper
154×185 cm
1993
photo: Tom Haartsen,
Ouderkerk a/d/Amstel

In dreams begin responsibilities
pastel, pencil, charcoal on paper
178.5×119.5 cm
1989
photo: Hogers/Versluys,
Stedelijk Museum, Amsterdam

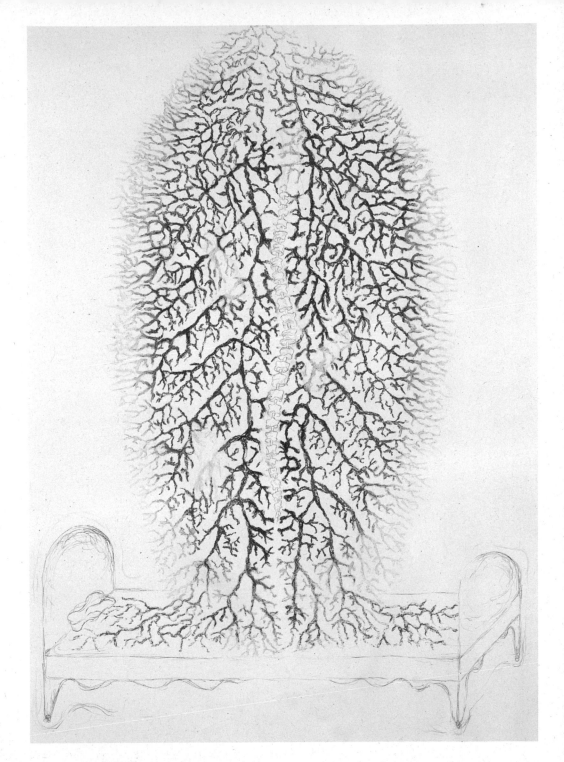

Dear...
still from film, 48 minutes, 16mm,
colour
written, directed and edited by
Ansuya Blom
camera and editing by Mark Glynne
cast: Anita Lotichius, Jacques
Commandeur, Renée Glynne
1998
photo: Mark Glynne, Amsterdam

Web III
printing ink, gouache pen on canvas
197×120 cm
1997
photo: Tom Haartsen, Ouderkerk
a/d/Amstel

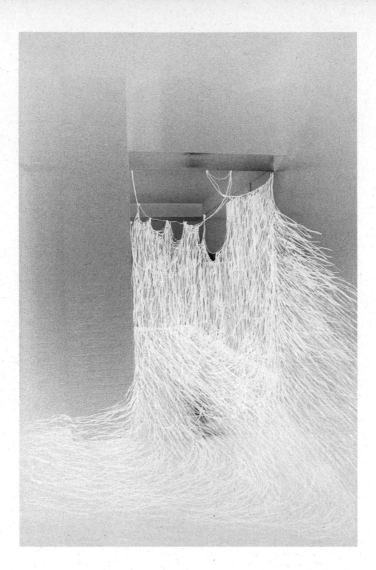

House of the invertebrates I – X
gouache pen
on ink-jet photographic prints
each 88 × 57 cm
2001

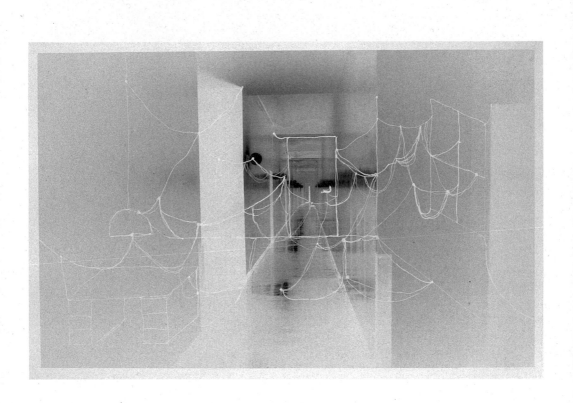

II

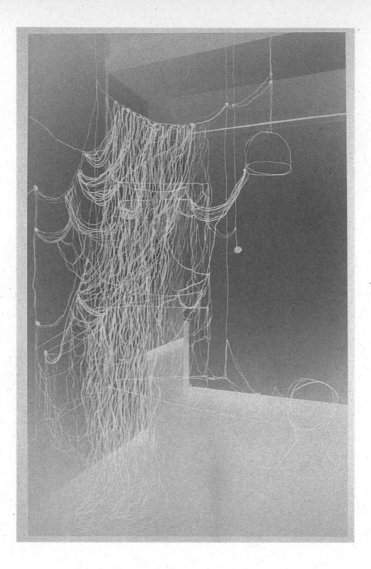

III

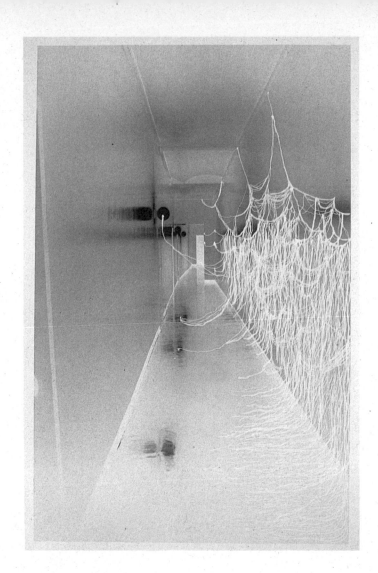

IV

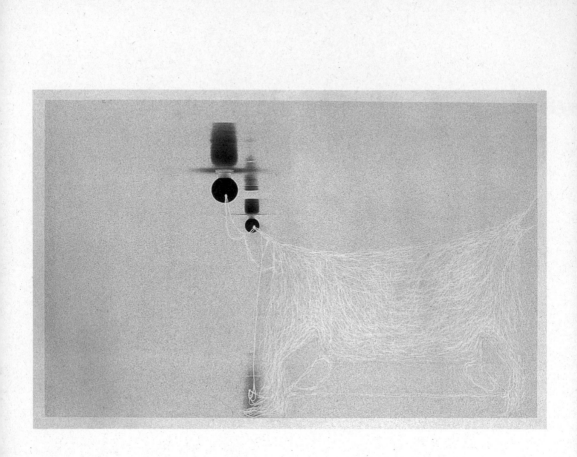

V

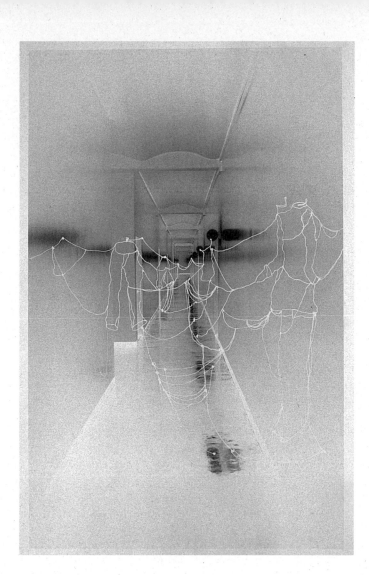

VI

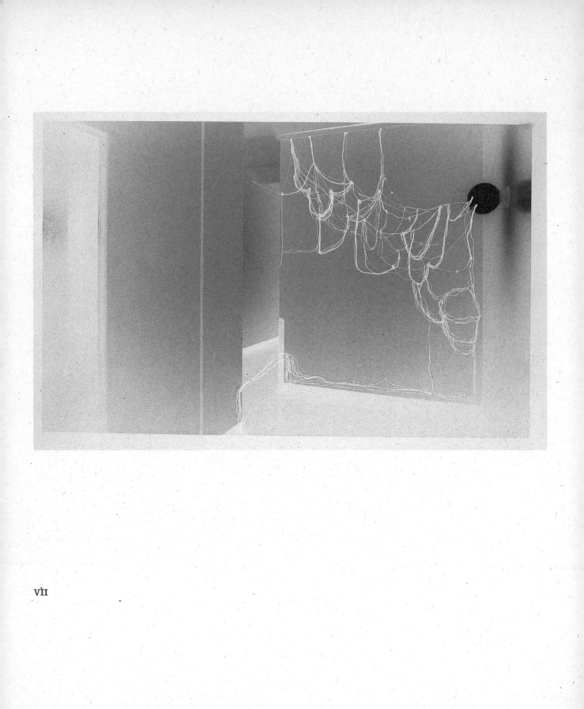

VII

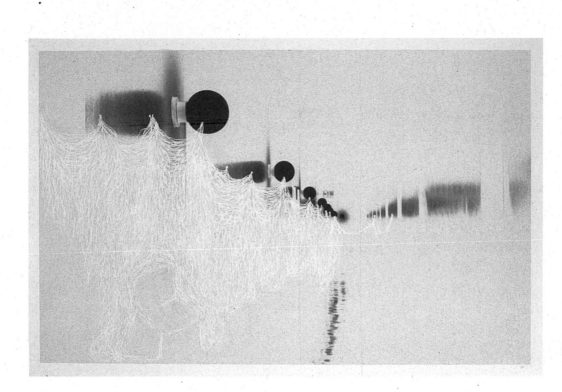

VIII

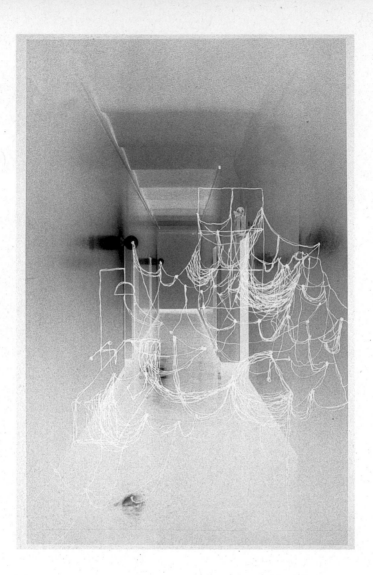

IX

X

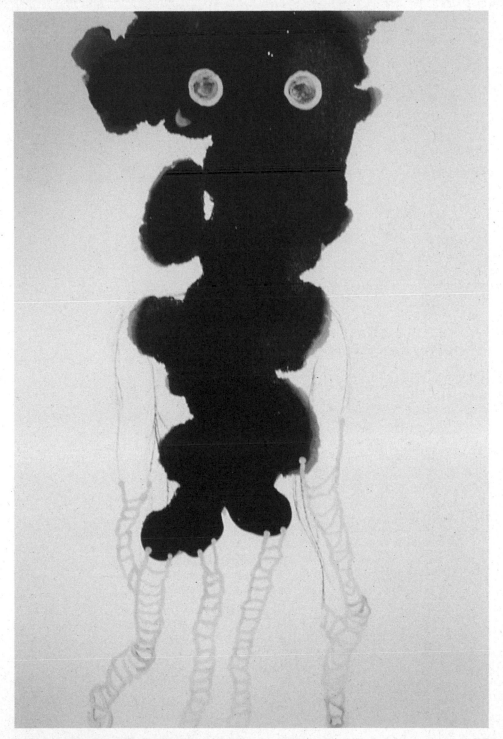

...daß dieser Mensch..., ink, gouache pen on photograph, 24 × 16 cm, 2001

Ansuya Blom's exhibition at the Centre for Drawing, February – March 2001

Michael Ginsborg:

You work in Amsterdam. Could you tell us what normal life is like, outside of the residency?

Ansuya Blom:

A complete contrast. One of the striking things I found being here is that once a week a group of students came to see me in my studio. Before I came here I thought 'I'm not sure this will be a good idea for me'. Usually, as an advisor at the Rijksakademie, I go to see the participant artists in their studios and we'll talk about their work, but they don't come to see mine. The other thing is that normally you can decide what you show and what you don't. It's a very strange thing after twenty years of working on my own to have unfamiliar people look at the pieces, good or bad, unresolved and at a very early stage. I thought that was good, you see. You are put on the spot. By contrast Amsterdam life is completely different. I don't often have people visiting me in my studio, and I rarely show work in progress and there are definitely no photographs taken in there.

As we try to develop the arguments for this project, we're asking 'what is it about drawing that merits a centre devoted to it? What is it that drawing can do?'

I can't give a global definition, but for me it was a liberating practice, because having been trained as an artist and having worked where painting was very dominant, in a country where painting holds a very big position, it became a very heavy weight. I just didn't know what to do with it. I was put into this tradition without really knowing why. The only thing could be that I was Dutch, which is no reason. What I find with drawing is that it is so simple. I like the idea that everybody can do it, this childish act. It's so close to the hand, this very direct contact with what you draw on, it maybe allows me to think while I draw. With painting I found a lot of things were standing behind me, watching me as I worked.

What are the worlds that drawing can reveal or enable that painting can't?

The basic qualities of drawing are very important to me. The fact that it relates to writing, as I enjoy reading very much. There are very close links from mind to hand to paper. You can have a visual description of an idea, or a literary description of an idea.

In the series *House of the invertebrates* that you have made here, you literally have both happening. A line comes in from the edge, then it goes into a kind of 'writing' in which an object is made in writing. And then the line goes off again.... Can you tell us more about the link between drawing and writing?

I've had this correspondence since I was here with a close friend of mine in Holland. He's been writing me letters every other day and so that forced me to write him letters. I would be making a little bit of a drawing and then I would move on to this letter describing to him what I had been doing and thinking about in this place, and then go back to the drawing. There is something about handwriting which comes very close to drawing.

When I was taught to write many years ago you had to draw the letters. You had to do your 'h' with a loop and come down and then go round and that's a drawn thing in a way. The fact that 'h' then becomes the first letter of the word 'hut' is another issue.

It's nice that you say 'drawn' because then you can just imagine drawing the ink out of the pen. In Dutch, *tekenen* is the word for drawing and *betekenis* is the word for meaning. So they are very closely linked to each other. The act of drawing is a way of giving meaning to the line that I am putting onto the paper.

So the line is very charged, it's a sign, it's got potential for you?

On canvas I can draw and then rub out, but on a piece of paper that is impossible, especially with the gouache pen drawings I have done here. Once the pen hits the paper that mark will be there, and there is something challenging about having to be so specific, and trying not to be too specific, because if you are too specific it is not interesting. I don't want to make something that I know I'm making, I want to make something that I don't know that I'm making.

You want to discover something?

Yes. To come back to writing again, maybe this is something I rediscovered in writing the letters to my friend. When you are writing to someone who is close to you, you write things which you normally wouldn't voice, confidential things.

Can you tell us a bit more about the *House of the invertebrates* drawings?

I came here with prints made from photographs that I'd made while visiting a site in New York. They were snapshots, just for me to remember this place because I was planning to do something with it, although I had no idea what exactly. When I was asked to come here and look at the space at the Centre for Drawing, there was something that clicked and I decided to use these photographs. I reworked them and had them printed on a special kind of paper. And then I just used a very ordinary white gouache graphics pen.

So the decision to use the photographs didn't come about until you were in the space here?

No. I knew that it was too short a time to come here completely blank.

The actual photograph, though, is reversed?

Yes, and the colour is changed.

So quite a lot of things have happened to the photographs.

Yes, I work with an ordinary colour copy machine, I've changed the colours to my taste and reworked them; darkened or lightened them, made them brighter.

The more I've thought about the drawings, the more I've thought of the two stages, the photographic part and the drawing part. And I've been thinking about what a corridor is, it's a kind of no-man's land. The rooms are where people actually are living their lives, not in the corridor. The corridor is a passage, a transitional space, a space you move through. You have no interest in it, except to get to somewhere else. I think of passages, rites of passage.

Well not for me! It's more that I'm trying to imagine what could be behind those walls. That was my initial idea, but it became a very rigid idea. There comes a point when the work says 'No! I want you to do something else'. At first, I was interested

in the spaces behind the wall, but then I was interested in moving into the corridor, as a space we stay in.

Certainly, when you look at them you stay in the space, but what also interested me was the two stages: the given photographic element, where you've done this reversal, and the drawing part.

The photographic reworking is just a beginning. Then maybe I have to draw in order to attack that image.

I was thinking about drawing as a way of inhabiting the image.

Yes, as a projection, yes absolutely.

I think of these lines as a substitute for touch, almost a sort of sensing through drawing. They are like a journey up the corridor, a sensing out of what you've actually got in the photograph.

Yes they are. Because I did touch. This is what I like about drawing, at times, the way it starts to lead its own life. This is what I meant when I said there comes a point when the drawing says 'I don't want this, do something else'...

You mean making a world, and then that world taking over what you've made and saying it has to go another way?

Yes.

I suppose the drawings that are the most sensational really, although I don't think necessarily they are the most beautiful, are these ones where the line multiplies. I was really intrigued as to why some drawings stayed very sparse and why some have begun to get very dense and quite threatening in a way. Something is happening here which if I was in that corridor.... Someone who's written about your work has mentioned David Lynch and *Blue Velvet*.

I wasn't very happy with that. I really don't like that film very much. But you know I'm not responsible for his associations.

But there is an eeriness about this. It's not a walking or touching kind of line, but it actually becomes a kind of mist, a miasma. You wonder if it could be a kind of poisonous emanation. I thought it was wonderful that you could actually move from drawings which were very thin armatures, to denser drawings that could take on the connotation of a kind of mist, a vapour.

Well, I can't comment on that because you never know the way something works.

It's always what people want to know about though.

Yes, but once you really start to know about it, this is when you should get really worried. It's not about wanting to be ignorant. It's more a case of allowing the image to be there, instead of really understanding why it came about. Those are two different things. It's happened to me so many times that I've come into my studio and thought this means this, and then a year later I think something else entirely. It can mean paralysis to be too sure of what things mean.

Question from the audience:
Ansuya, I notice that you said the original pale blue photographs were reversals. They were drawn on with a white line, so is that also a reversal of a black line?

That's a very good question. Why white? I was just fed up with black. It sounds totally blunt but black became an effort, and maybe it just seemed to hamper something. I'm not sure what it is, but I just needed to do something else.

I like the white but then it occurred to me that if you reversed it it would probably have quite a different look.

Yes, it would. I might try that now, now that I have done this.

Are your drawings works in themselves or are they preparations for something else?

That's something I don't know. It's happened a lot with work that I start with something and then it moves into something else. So for example I've made a series of drawings called *...daß dieser Mensch...* which is translated as 'this human being'. They are drawn on photographs that come from stills from a film that I made. So first I made the film, then I decided the film wasn't finished so I did this drawing on the wall. Then we filmed that and put it in the film. Then I took a picture of that drawing and now I am using the photograph and I keep changing the colours. I don't know. I can't answer that question.

When I first looked at slides of your drawings, I thought perhaps it was a drawing of light. As someone working in drawing, and with photography and film, what do you think about the relationship between those different media?

I would say that I just do drawings and films.
I use a photograph as a base for my drawings,
but I don't see myself as a photographer. They are
still very much drawings, just with the use of a

photographic image. Photography is an area I
really don't know anything about. With these
images it's like buying a newspaper and drawing
over the newspaper pages. I take maybe a little
bit longer to get this particular 'newspaper', but
that's how I feel that it sits. The difference
between the drawings and the films is maybe
where the writing comes in. Often I start writing
a text, and from the text comes the film, because
there is something compelling enough for me to
say 'well I have to do something with this text'.
That's as vague as it is when it starts, using a text
is something that I rarely do within a drawing.
It's also about wanting to do something in a
specific period of time. Not in terms of the making
of the work, but in terms of the way a film has a
beginning and an end. It's similar in a way to
when a drawing moves into a piece of writing.

The work of Ansuya Blom is rich in its material evocativeness and facture, its content, and most of all its abiding sense of the complexity of the mind's processing of its moods and understandings. It makes use of different strategies also – collaboratively made films as well as a steady practice in the studio. But whatever the form her work finally takes, a communicative pressure is felt that can at times resemble the receiving or the finding of a letter; the narration of the film *Dear...* makes particular use of the letter form, though leaving the addressee and the writer of the letters unlocated and unnamed. When considering Blom's work, the important questions are those of its meaning, for when communicative and expressive urgency is found in an artist's work, our first thoughts are, what is it that is being expressed? And the situation which governs what we consider the meanings to be is not simple. It could be said that her works excavate a potential space for communication and intimacy within a public sphere regarded at best with suspicion and sometimes (in the letters of the film *Dear...* , for example, though they cannot be regarded as a proxy figure for the artist's own views) as an outright source of hostility, force and insinuation. Although her working life has been mostly in a western democratic state, it is significant that amongst European literature the artist has had cause to revisit Georg Büchner's fable of the soldier-murderer Woyzeck, and also the story of Kaspar Hauser, which gave rise to the series of drawings titled *...daß dieser Mensch...* (begun in 1992). Both stories return us to doubts about the reach of European and Enlightenment definitions of humanity.[1]

One factor governing the overall meaning of Blom's work is that the freedom I sense is being defended can never be a fixity. It is an inescapable aspect of freedoms won (and enjoyed) in such different domains as law, thought, speech or art that they can also be lost and eroded; they therefore require a constant effort of nurture and vigilance. That counts as common knowledge outside the overdeveloped countries, but is not always so present to thought within them.[2]

Ansuya Blom's exhibition at the Centre for Drawing, February – March 2001

How to connect the theme of freedom with Blom's works themselves and their methods? The sense of transience in her drawings and her use of unorthodox materials – making drawings by means of the destructive properties of flame, for example, in a series from 1993, *The mute house* – might be interpreted not according to unknowable speculations about personal psychology, or even with reference to the changing rhetorical role of gesture, authenticity and mark-making in recent art, but in relation to that basic provisionality and unfixity of freedom, both psychological or political. It is the very affecting intimacy of Blom's achievements that causes me to argue here for a sense of their wider political situation. But a strain is evident in this attempt at assigning a single strong meaning to the sense of impermanence in the drawings. The formal continuities in Blom's work would need to be looked at more closely before such an interpretation could be made. It is never inappropriate to defer, for a little while, the discussion of meaning in order to see where a concentration on formal questions – spatial conventions for example – leads. Discussion of meaning in art, though essential, leaves us too frequently bereft of agreement, and may lead to a somewhat despairing sense that meaning must be irrevocably consigned to the realm of private speculation; 'private' in the withered sense that anything goes, rather than that a fullness of perception or expression has successfully been conserved within larger strictures.

The series of works made by Ansuya Blom during her residency at Wimbledon is a good place to think more deeply about some formal aspects of her art – and about some distinctions between different understandings of drawing. The first thing to say about these drawings, all given the title *House of the invertebrates*, is that they are made on the surface of ink-jet images derived from photographs of corridors, printed in a single blue-grey, not quite the colour of architectural blueprints, and in negative. These are drawn on with a white gouache pen, and the gouache is absorbed a little into the matt surface of the prints; you have a sense that the line binds with the material structure of the paper, while remaining visually distinct from the photographic image it makes use of. Windows, a desk, hanging light fixtures, beds, baths, sinks, clothing and plumbing are visible, often linked together as though with hanging threads, though some works (no. X, for example) lack any specific objects and simply employ a swathe of drawn lines, almost resembling fur or hair. Drawings made with flame have already been mentioned; these works use an unfamiliar white line which frequently suspends itself or makes connection with the dark areas of the prints. So there are questions of how lines relate to light – a light switch itself is visible in no. III. Perhaps there is a Beuysian sense that drawing is being used to dramatise areas of energy: the dark source areas are often lights in the original corridor, and in negative their energy has become a paradoxical 'dark light'. But it is more basic questions about drawing I want to focus on.

First, think about how drawings may represent space. Imagine you are making a drawing of a room and its furnishings. How would you start? Most probably with an idea of space described by the conventions of perspective, in which the crucial factor is that the space taken up by solid objects and bodies is accorded an equal value as that taken by the air between them. Nevertheless, in grappling with the communicative function of drawing, you would be likely to exaggerate the size of solid forms, or at least we could say that you would use them as the way of locating the space around and between them – unless, as in many Renaissance paintings, there was a handy checker-board marble floor to do a lot of that work for you. *The House of the invertebrates* drawings are somewhere between perspectival space (they hang themselves on the camera's automated version of it) and a depiction of space that admits evidence of other senses than the eye, notably touch. The separate objects and fixtures that make up these lived-in, domestic spaces are unusual in that they are connected and traversed by lines that sometimes hang as threads or string would, obeying gravity and falling in loops, and sometimes follow more obscure paths. Here is another way of representing solid bodies and the space between them, and through these interconnecting lines, not through the usual resort to obviously architectural lines of recession or checker-board floors. The drawings do not simply pose tactile or pre-perspectival space against camera-recorded space, the tactile against the ocular; they make their own convention for space, and it is post-perspectival, overlaying the view of the camera.

Return to the decisions that you make when drawing. To draw any bounded object within space, most of us would jump immediately to the decision of what kind of line to use – hesitant, broken, feathery or firm. But this is actually to skip a stage of decision-making we may not realise we are making, which is whether or not to draw using outlines at all. Our drawings would turn out feathery or firm, but they would nearly all depend on the convention of outlines. Outlines have a purpose and our experience of objects as bounded is reasonably expressed by using them. Diagrams, on the other hand, make use of a purer mathematical precision, or use conventions that mean we can reconstruct what is depicted without ambiguity, or sometimes drastically simplify, neglecting outlines for inner structure. They have a different kind of objectivity, and a useful one, but tend to omit the sensual aspects of space. If you look closely at Ansuya Blom's drawings, you will see that in some respects at least, they are closer to diagrams than to outline drawings. Of course it would be hard to reconstruct their spaces, especially as, quite unlike diagrams, they often demonstrate a need to go over a line with many many others – though it should be pointed out that this is not done in a spirit of revising or approximation, or as though drawing from observation. The diagrammatic approach can be seen in how when drawing the pipe that leads to a shower-head, for example, she uses one line to depict the hollow pipe, not two. It's the idea-aspect of the thing rather than the visual experience of the thing. Although the overall effect is very often tactile and delightfully so because of the quality of the line and the conventions for making space used, at the level of the most basic decision-making we are in the realm of the diagram rather than an outline drawing from observation: we are in a mental space, but one that has sensual aspects.

Form is properly considered as 'inner content', and was defined as such in German Romanticism. In any art that engages us form and content can never be fully separated, though for purposes of discussion we can train ourselves to think about them independently. Beyond the type of space made in this new series, and the kinds of line used, line does here take on a meaning of its own; it becomes a motif. There is not so much modern art that makes use of Blom's kind of line, that is simultaneously idea and embodiment; one example that could be looked at in comparison would be the white lines that organise the black and red areas in an early work by Philip Guston, *The Tormentors* (1947–8, San Francisco Museum of Art). The space there is much flatter, but the lines have an ability to change their meaning: now stitching, now describing a cowl or the sole of a shoe, while always demonstrating the involvement of figures in the space around and between them. Line in Guston's early work does become content, though never entirely, and the motifs in Guston's late works are not separable from the continuing drama of how those works were made; they represented no apostasy from what he had learnt as an abstract artist. Blom's repertoire of identifiable motifs is, like Guston's, not large; but the meanings of the motifs are continually inflected in a comparable way.

Whatever comparisons we bring to Ansuya Blom's *House of the invertebrates* series, and whatever meanings, finally, we think her work expresses, I hope this account has said enough to indicate howsome formal questions in her work can be looked at, with a view to the theme of freedom, mental and political. By realising that the consensual, shared space of linear perspective is not finally cast off or wholly rebelled against in these works, we can begin to see how the strong ability to invite the viewer into a particular world – not, perhaps, any longer merely a 'personal' world, but one demonstrating awareness of others, and of other forces – is arrived at.

Ian Hunt

Ian Hunt writes on art – most recently on Pamela Golden, Aaron Williamson, Lily Markiewicz, Mark Wallinger – and is the publisher of the poetry imprint Alfred David Editions, which publishes Hunt's story *The Daubers* in English and German, as part of a collaborative book with the Swiss artist Andreas Rüthi, *Still Life Paintings*.

1 Woyzeck (see John Reddick's translation for the Penguin Büchner) is referred to by the artist in the interview with Stuart Morgan in Ansuya Blom, *Let me see, if this be real* (NAi Publishers, Rotterdam, 1999), in the context of a discussion of irrational commands that must be obeyed. Motifs that recall Woyzeck are to be found in several of Blom's works. Kaspar Hauser, the sixteen-year-old who stumbled into Nuremberg in 1828, having been raised in virtual darkness since the age of four, is a much debated case in the literature of language acquisition and psychology; but his murder in 1832 was also significant, and was described by Anselm Ritter von Feuerbach, the German jurist who first wrote up the story, as constit-uting a whole new category of crime, 'soul murder'.

2 Another way of raising some of these questions would be to point to the difficulties involved in assigning Blom's work to a tradition of Dutch art, and to make clear how inter-national it is in awareness and sympathies: jazz, blues, Cree and Sioux poetry. See also *Ansuya Blom* (Ikon Gallery, Birmingham, 1994), and Stuart Morgan, 'The Secret Life of Belly and Bone' in *What the Butler Saw*, ed. Ian Hunt (Durian, London, 1996), reprinted from the Stedelijk Museum catalogue of 1990.

Alexander Roob lives and works in Düsseldorf, Germany. Born in Laumersheim, he studied art at the Hochschule Künste, Berlin, from 1977 to 1985. As well as being an artist, he has worked as a cartoonist, muralist and stage-designer; he has also translated some of the late poems of William Blake into German.

Since 1985 Alexander Roob has produced seven chapters of CS, a long-term drawing project, working immediately on site in various locations that have attracted his interest. He has exhibited this work in galleries and museums in many parts of Europe, among others at the Städtische Galerie im Lenbachhaus, Munich (1998), the Graphische Sammlung Albertina, Vienna (1999), and most recently at the Museum für Moderne Kunst in Frankfurt (2000) and the Goethe Institut in Rotterdam (2000). His exhibition at the Centre for Drawing in summer 2001 was his first in the UK. He has received several awards and scholarships, including a DAAD Stipendium in 1986 and a Rome Scholarship in 1996.

Five CS books (CS I-III to CS VII) have been published to accompany Alexander Roob's exhibitions. He has also written theoretical books including *Alchemy and Mysticism, the Hermetic Museum* (Benedikt Taschen, Cologne 1996) and *Theorie des Bildromans* (Villa Massimo/ Salon Verlag, Rome/Cologne 1997).

Alexander Roob is currently Professor of Drawing at the Hochschule für Bildende Kunst in Hamburg. He is represented by Galerie Ursula Walbröl, Düsseldorf, and Galerie Anita Beckers, Frankfurt.

The form of drawing I prefer is utterly tactile. By drawing, I release myself from rigid perception and transpose things into flowing, rhythmic processes. It is an almost blind act of feeling which disregards the substantive and focuses on the relational. Drawing reacts seismographically to the specific tensions of different events and locations. The lines in a drawing I produce in an operating theatre have a completely different character to those in a drawing made at the stock exchange.

A more fluid and physical relationship with reality starts to develop in this way through drawing – and I think ideas of perception have changed fundamentally in this direction. The way I see it, photography and film, those constrained and contracted visual media, no longer work properly.

Alexander Roob, April 2001

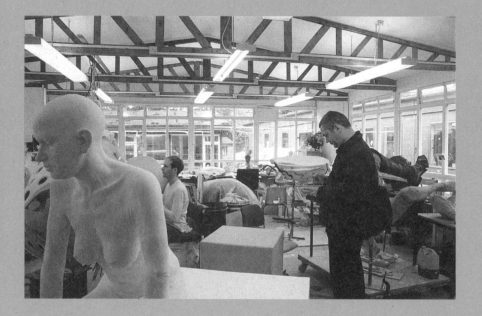

Alexander Roob drawing in the theatre design studios at Wimbledon School of Art, May 2001

Alexander Roob editing his drawings in the Centre for Drawing, May 2001

CS – Protocol: Wimbledon School of Art
charcoal pencil on paper
each drawing 15 × 21 cm
2001

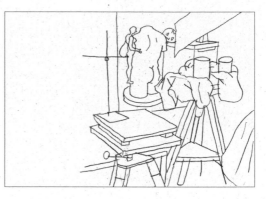

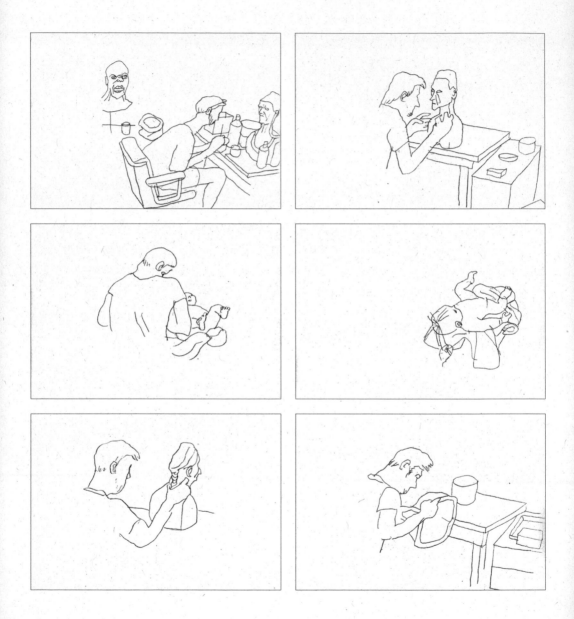

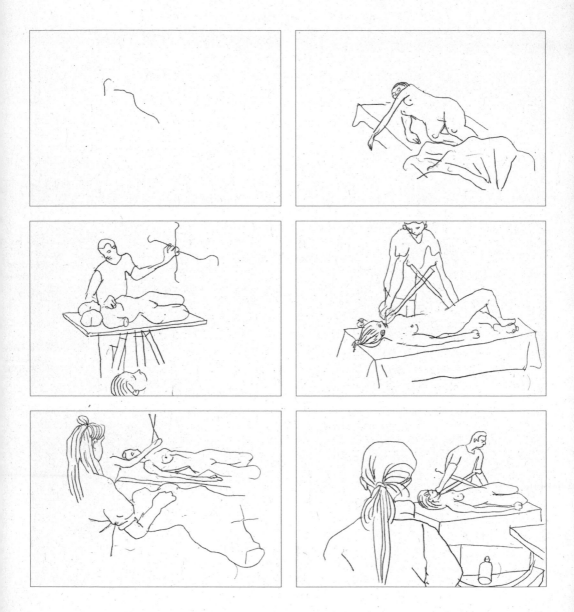

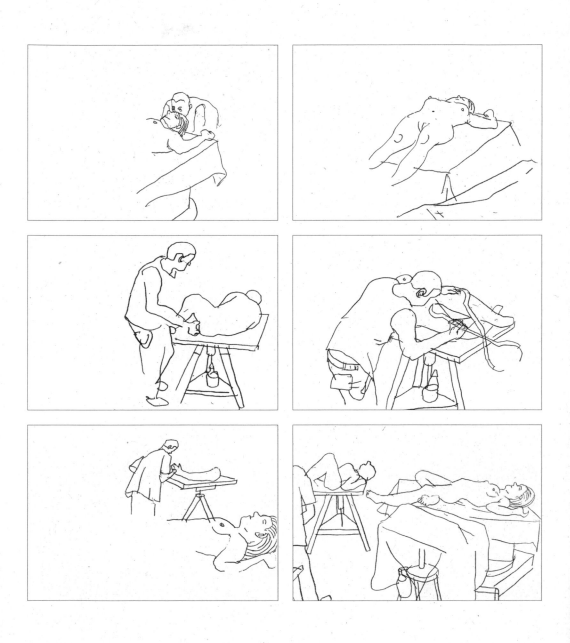

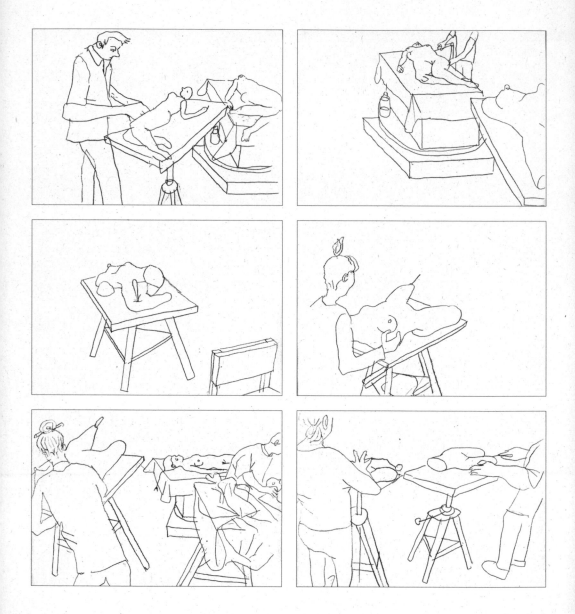

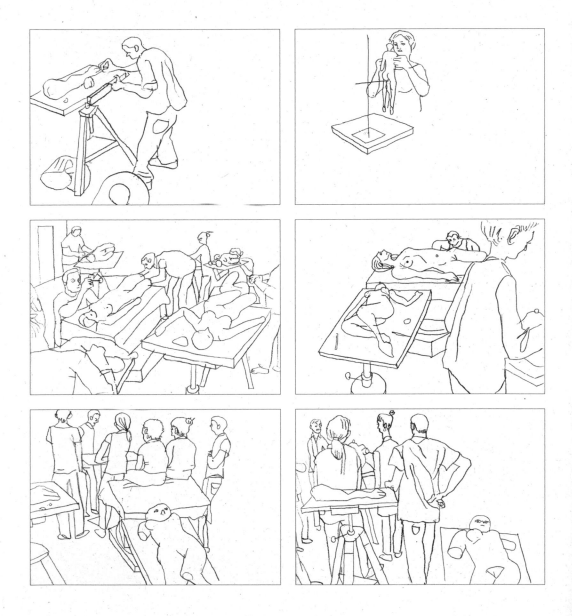

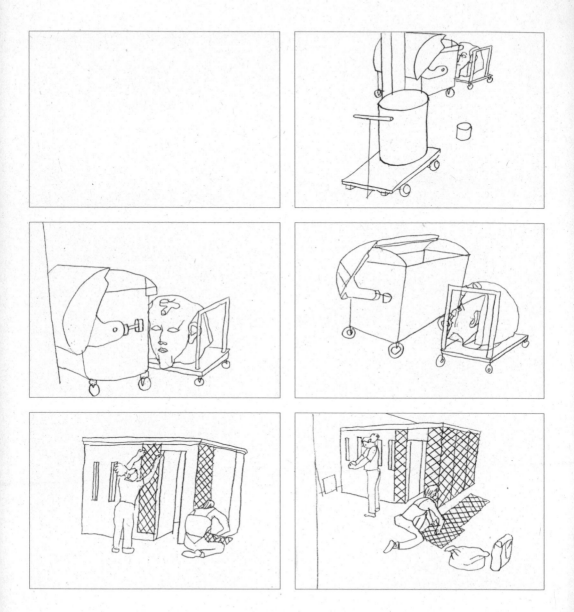

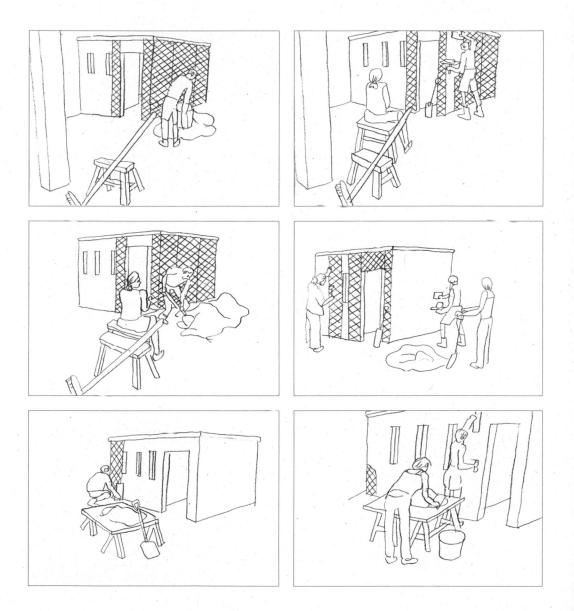

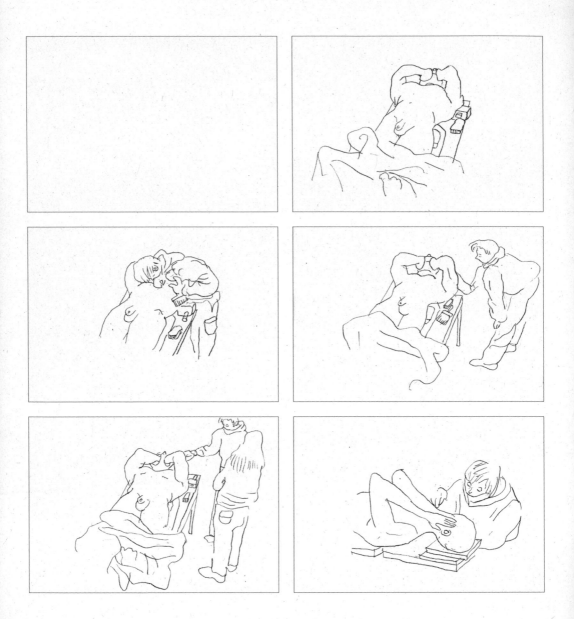

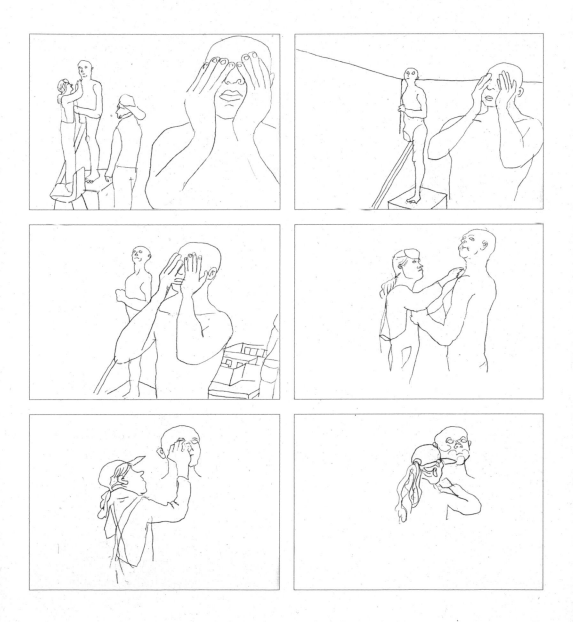

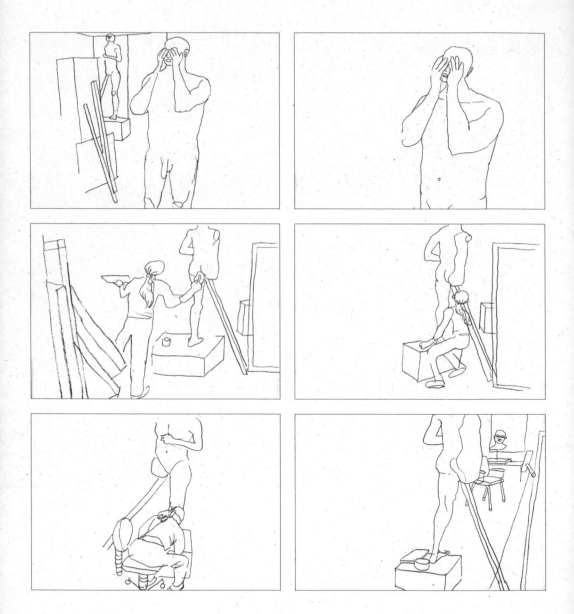

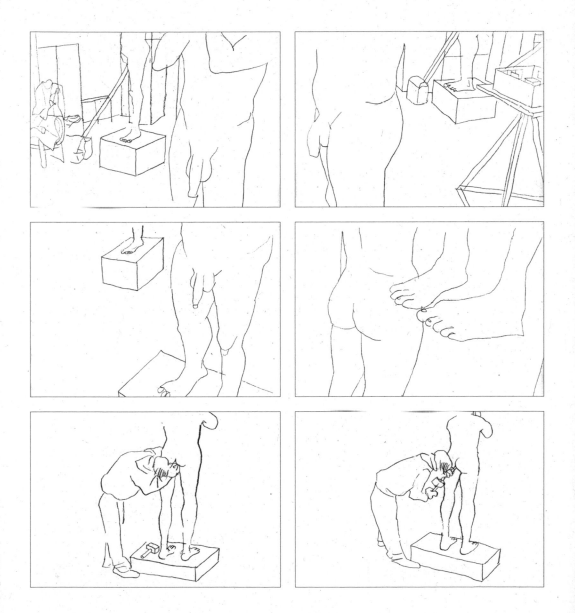

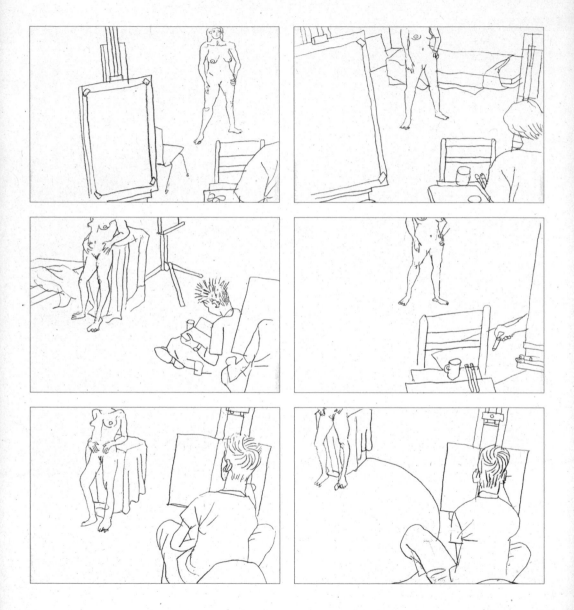

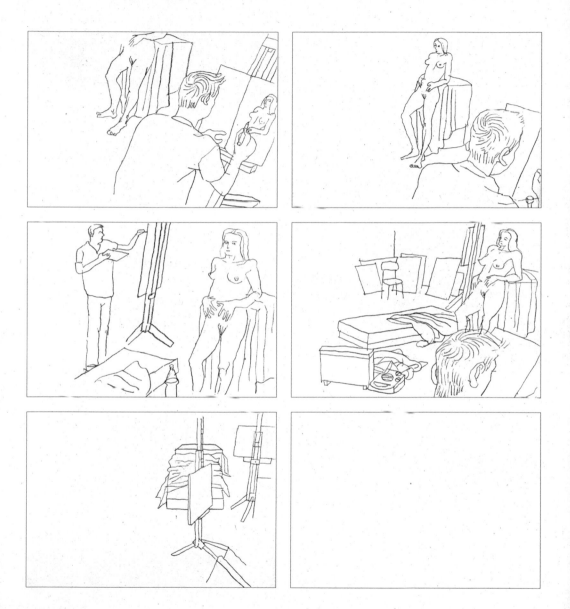

117

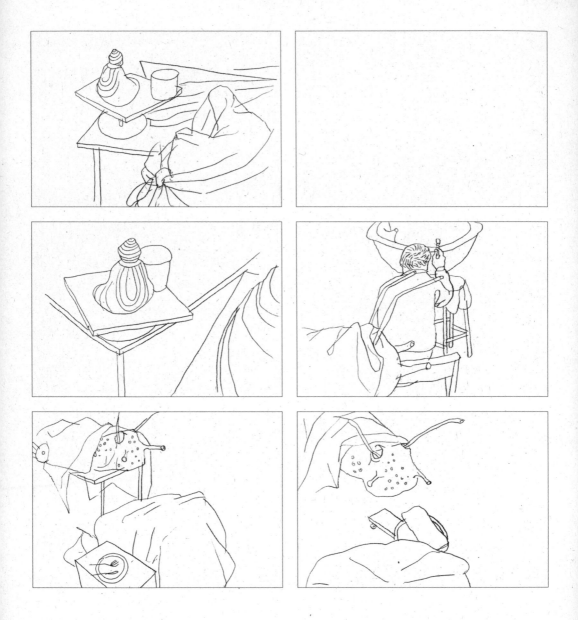

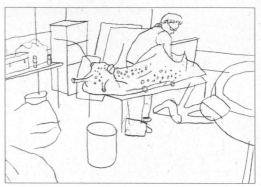

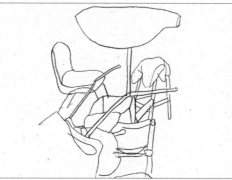

121

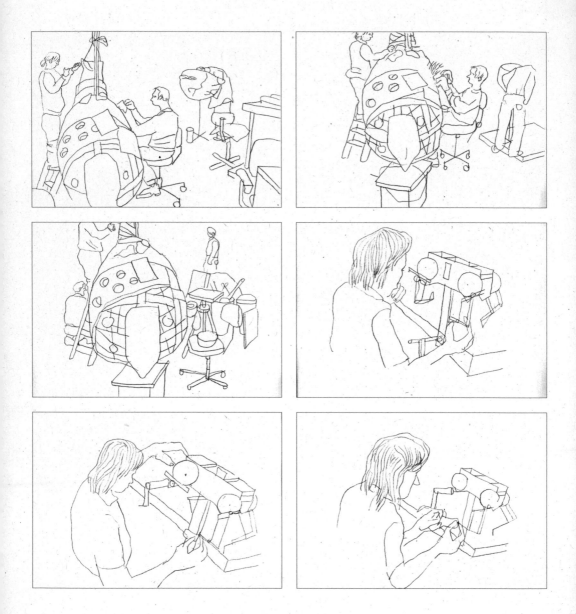

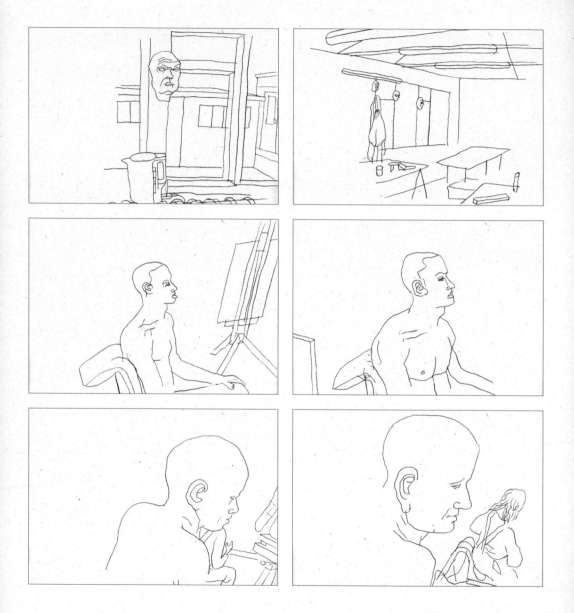

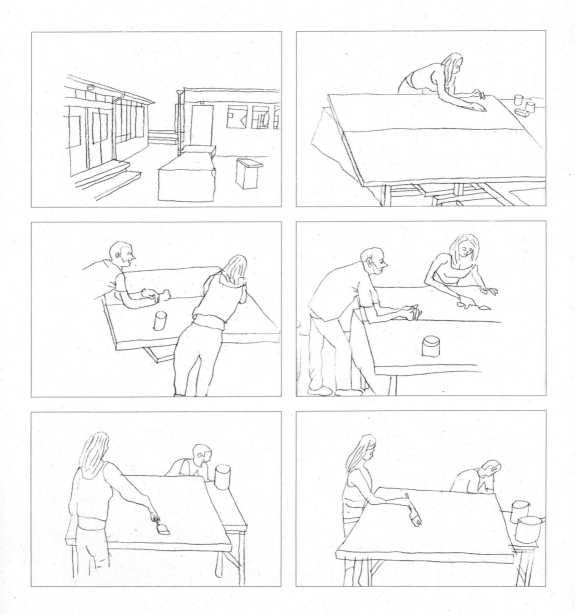

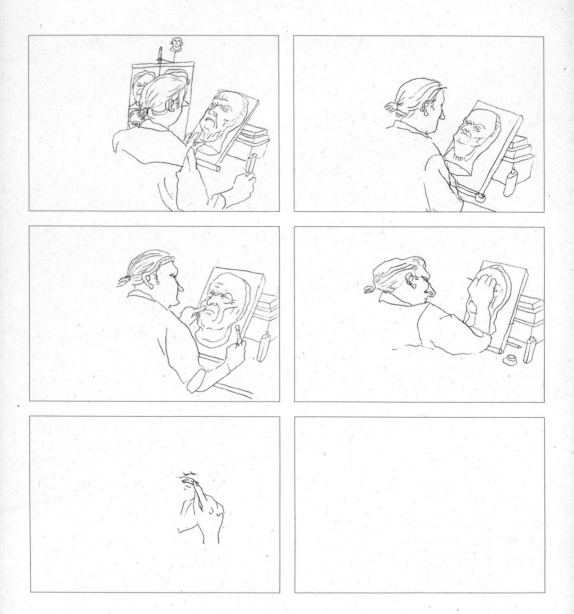

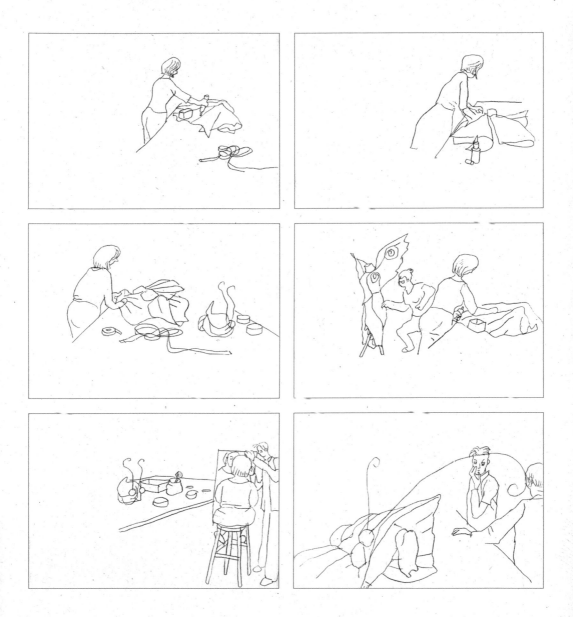

127

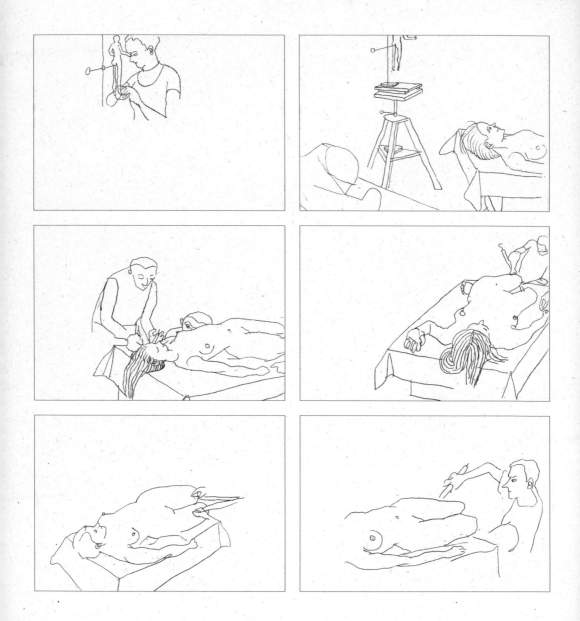

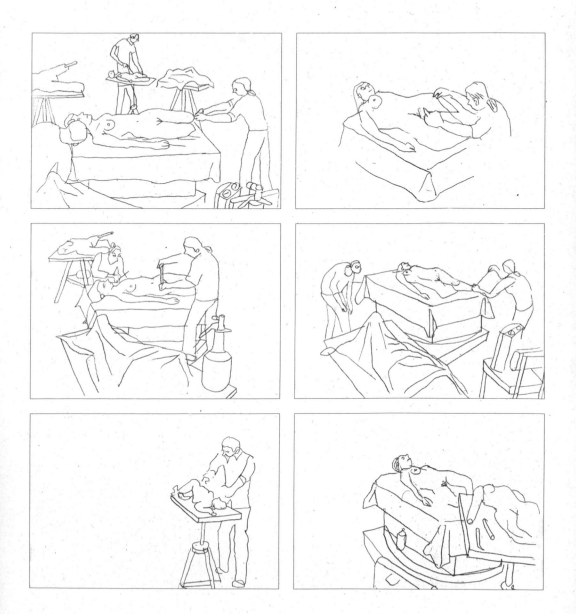

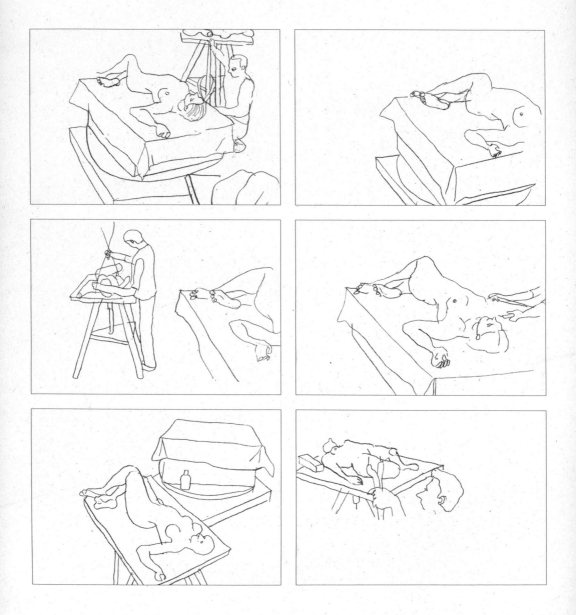

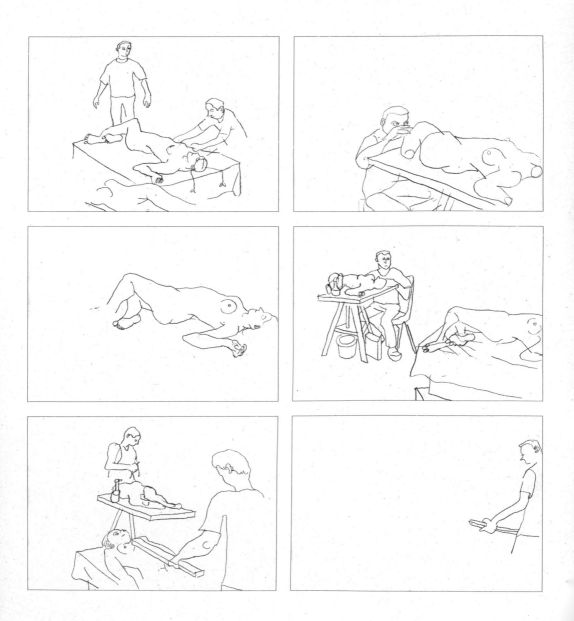

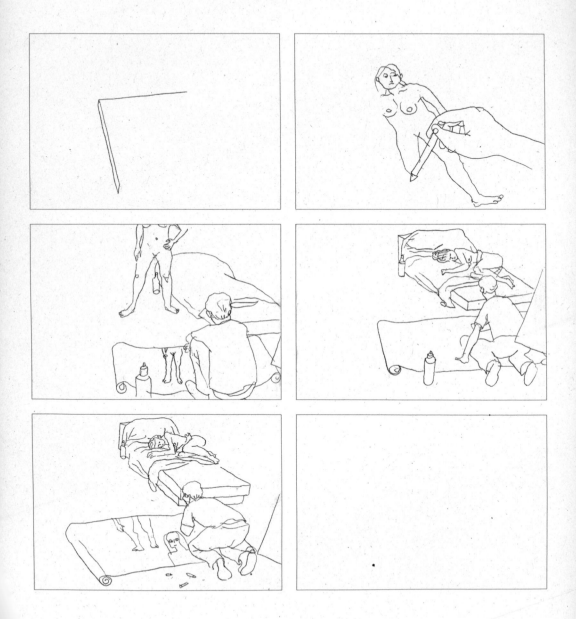

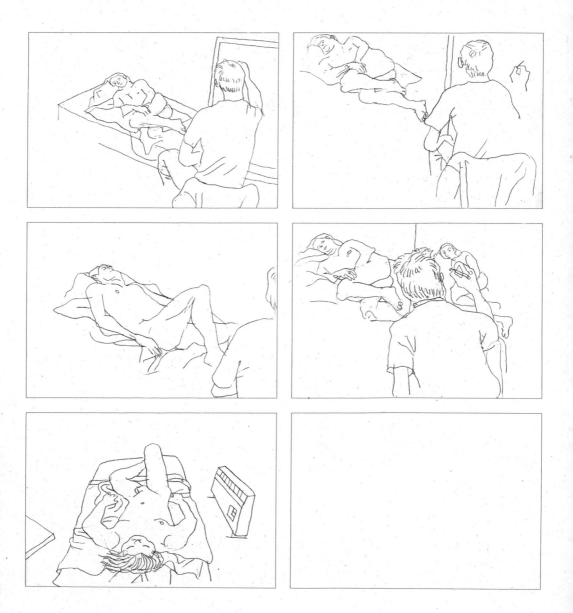

135

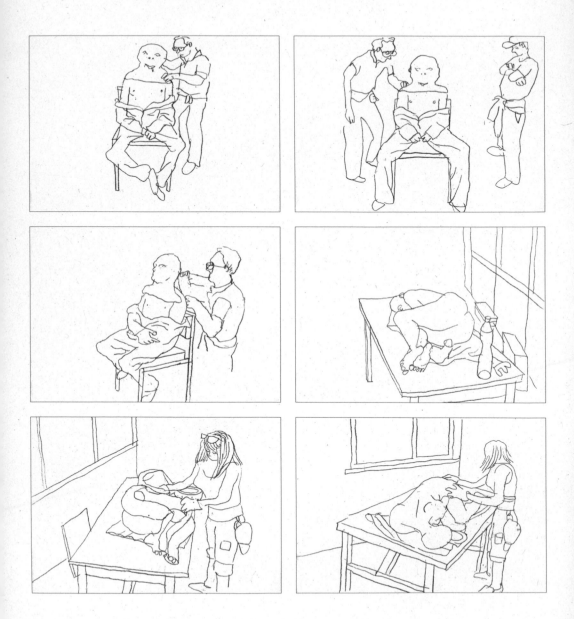

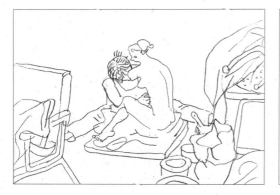

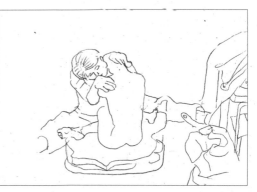

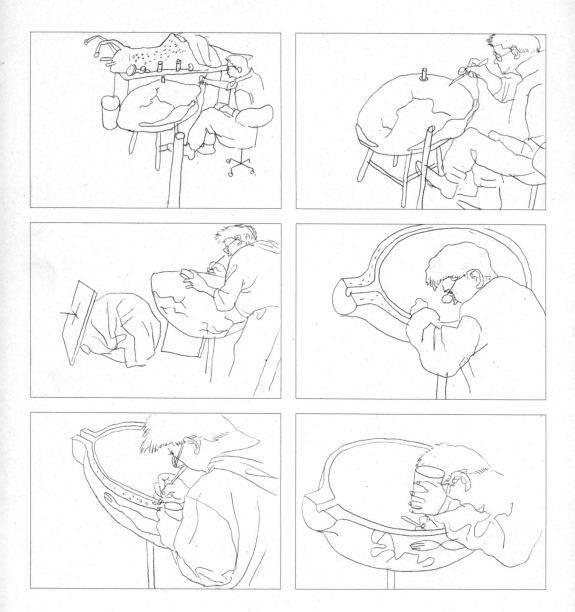

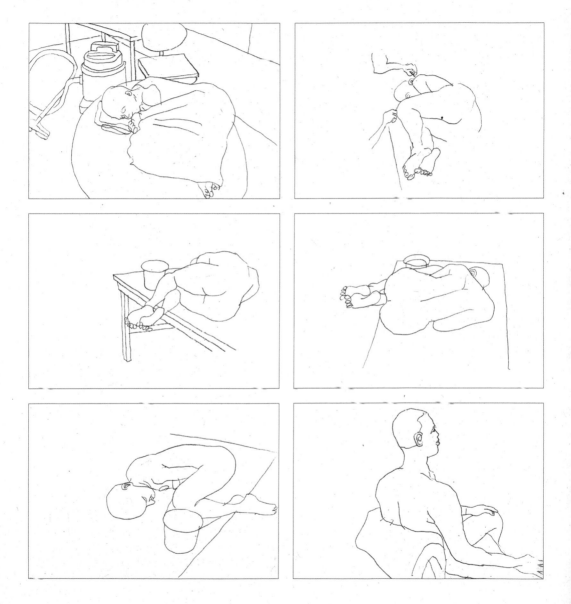

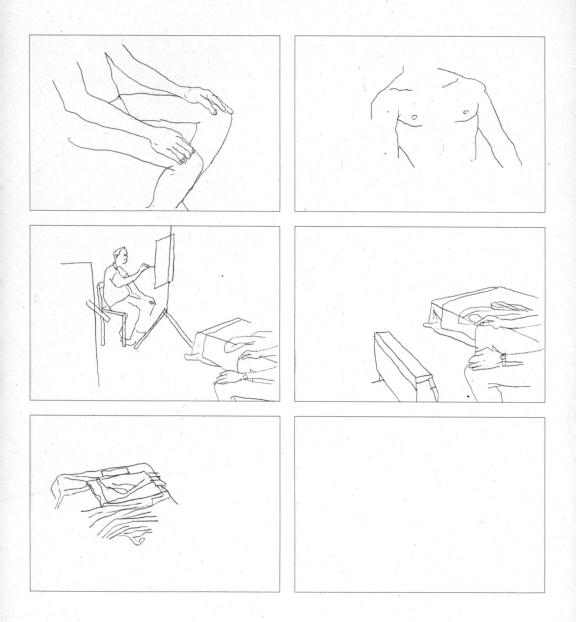

Alexander Roob's exhibition at the Centre for Drawing, June – July 2001

Kate Macfarlane:

Your usual role in an art school is as a teacher. How have you found your role here as artist-in-residence?

Alexander Roob:

I decided to go back to school again, as a student. When I first visited Wimbledon we exchanged publications. The one I received contained an interesting article about the 'death of life drawing'.[1] I thought, if drawing in the life room today is so outdated that it becomes nearly impossible to do, that's the point at which to start anew with it. In Hamburg, where I teach drawing, I experiment with new possibilities for life drawing, with elements of theatre and action. Everything is put in motion, the models, the students, the whole situation is fluid. It's a bit like musical chairs. A few weeks before I came here I suggested to the students that we try to work with a nude model, and they replied, 'anything but that'. So I took the opportunity of working in the life room at Wimbledon.

The students were not interested in life drawing?

No, not in this classical way of life drawing with a nude in the centre, which is the incarnation of boring academicism – and has the problem of anthropocentric humanism, the idea of man as the measure of everything. If in the English language 'life drawing' means drawing the human body, that suggests the whole problem.

But isn't the way the life model is used in the theatre design studios quite different? We see students making very accurate measurements of the figure.

Yes, this measuring. It's very strange. At the beginning of the residency I showed some slides as an introduction to my ideas about drawing. Among them were two famous works by William Blake, a visionary portrait of Newton and one of the demiurge, Urizen. Both of them include a pair of compasses as a symbol of the limitation of liveliness by the reasoning mind. It was a big surprise to find these very instruments in the theatre technical arts life room, being used to measure the living forms of the nude model. I don't know if sculptors in Blake's time also used this technique.

One thing I noticed in the drawings is that you see the students working directly from the figure, measuring; then you see them chiselling and sawing and you realise that they are working on their own versions of the figure. There's much more concentration on the figure in these drawings than in those made in other locations.

Every location has a new challenge. For me, here, it was the human body. In previous drawings my understanding of the human figure was more as a marionette, to avoid any hierarchy in the field of perception.

So that the figures have an equal weighting to everything around them? In your drawings the architecture and objects do seem to coalesce with the figures, they're all treated in the same manner.

Yes, and that is exactly the problem of the life room, its implied hierarchy. It's difficult to develop lively human figures that don't become the centre or focus of a drawing.

In these drawings the figures are often dramatic – I'm thinking of the masks. The figures created by the students actually do demand centre stage.

> Do you know the drawings I made recently in an operating theatre? These were in a way a preparation for the Wimbledon drawings. There are strong visual connections. What are the hands of the surgeon doing? What are the hands of the students doing? The whole space of the operating theatre drawings is defined by the gestures and interactions between communicating hands. It's very interesting that the German word for action, for the plot of a story or a film, is *Handlung*, from the word *Hand*. Action is what is done by the hand.

Often in your drawings, your drawing hand is present.

> There is one drawing in the Wimbledon series with this self-awareness of the drawing hand. I call this double attentiveness.

There's obviously a strong element of humour in the work. I noticed some people chuckling when we were looking at some of the drawings. Is this important to you?

> You mean the one where a female student hammers a chisel into the arse of a male statue? But I don't feel responsible for what the students are actually doing here. I think one reason for the humour is the outline's absence of concern for substance or material, which in a few cases causes confusion between the sculpturer and the sculpture. But I don't seek or resist humour; these strange and pithy moments exist, and I try to catch them as an angler catches a fish.

The work is very accessible, it enables everybody to comprehend what is presented, which must be one of the characteristics of drawing.

Drawing is usually regarded as a basic but subordinate medium, as a kind of foundation for developing ideas. But my intention is to use it as an independent and progressive medium in its own right. One advantage of drawing beside its immediate physicality is its economy – but this is also a problem. In comparison with the much wider possibilities of other media you are naked. You can't hide your inability under a veil of sounds and colours.

So why have you imposed on yourself the discipline of the outline?

I'm interested in ideas of perception and motion, but not in narration, like the author of a comic strip for example. More and more I've found that outline is the way to transform fixed items in motion. To make an outline drawing is for me a kind of musical act of feeling, which disregards the substantive and focuses on the relational. And it's also the result of an intensive period of time, of lively duration.[2]

This leads to the question of what kind of autonomy each individual drawing has.

I have absolutely no concept for a single drawing. But it's not like... in a comic strip for example, or a sequence of stills in a film. For me the real concern is a monad: that is, a minute unity of perception, which is also meant as a whole.[3] This moment in its complexity, this concrete situation incorporated in a certain perspective or point of view – Whitehead called these autonomous particles 'events'. For me every single drawing is such a particle or event. In my book, *Theory of the Drawn Novel*[4] I call them pulses of perception.

The book was actually inspired by William Blake and by the 'minute unities' in the philosophy of Whitehead.[5] The late poetry of Blake and the cosmology of Whitehead both contain a fundamental analysis of the outline and the creative act itself. These issues are for me quite involved ones. But you could say that every single particle or drawing of the CS project is complete in itself and also open on all sides.[6] There is an element in the line itself that points beyond the limitations of the single drawing and connects each with the surrounding ones.

Presumably the other reason for the use of drawing is that it enables you to slip back and forth between different states of consciousness almost, so that one frame may be representing your internal thoughts, while the next is an exact representation of what you perceive. Though in the Wimbledon drawings there seems to be a lot more from observation, and less introspection than before.

That's right. The direction of my work at the moment is an exterior one. The concepts for drawing in the last century were mostly interior ones: drawing as an auto-therapeutic secret code for example, expressionism and individual mythologies, perhaps also much concept art and the circular games of Fluxus. I think it's time for drawing to get more self-confidence and to come out of these hiding places. I am convinced that drawing is able to compete with the technical media of photography and film.

So you're not interested in self-revelation?

No, I want to establish drawing as an exterior medium again. But there is a long development to this. The beginnings of the drawing project seventeen years ago were very much to do with self-revelation and symbolism, with abstract signs and secret meanings. The first section of CS was the so-called 'codex one'. After that came the drawn novel: the idea of connecting everything, of a totality, a network of criss-crossings of thoughts, fantasies and direct perception. But I'm not interested any more in the idea of such a universal totality and I'm moving away from that approach. Now I'm trying out various possibilities, mainly reports, though last year I drew a kind of crime story. I used the flat of a friend in Berlin, and worked at the same time with a model and with people out of my imagination, tuned in to the location. They murdered themselves – though the only obvious thing is a dead body swimming in the river Spree.

They murdered themselves, or each other?

There was a murder. But... if you work without language, without captions, then you can't really grasp what's going on.

Does this connect with your film collaboration with Georg Winter?

Very much. Georg Winter is a plastic artist who works with what he calls the Ukiyo-Camera System. It's a cybernetic system, which is mainly concerned with the corporeal experience of the process of film-making, with its different modes of perception rather than its results. Consequently his wooden cameras don't contain any film. I invited him to produce a drawn film with the students – a drawn film not an animated film. It's a collaboration between two tactile systems: the wooden cameras and the pencils. The production was really exciting. I used the budget for models to pay professional actors and to rent a few locations in the red light district of Hamburg.

So it's again a very direct physical relationship, whether it's between the person with the wooden camera and the actors, or the very physical act of making the drawings....

Yes, physicality is decisive, and also the transparency and vulnerability of the drawing process, which enables it to reflect the specific tensions of different locations and situations. It's a kind of objectivity that technical media can only dream of. The box of the camera is in itself a bunker which needs to be overcome and abandoned.

One project we hope to organise is for you to work in the offices of a daily national newspaper, accompanying reporters and photographers to make drawings. Do you see your work as a form of reportage?

It is, but I come back to this film project: the main character is a blind photographer. I think if what I do is reporting, it's a kind of blind reporting, without or before language. Perhaps it's comparable in some way to the ideas of the hermetic philosophers of a language without preconceptions, the myth of the language of Adam in paradise, where the name and the thing are absolutely identical. But it's a fluid language, a language of process, and it connects also with Wilhelm Busch's idea of the 'liquefying of situation'. I was astonished, speaking to the students here, to find out that hardly anyone knows of Wilhelm Busch in Britain.[7] He's an artist who is as important as William Hogarth or Hokusai, with a very interesting philosophical background.

If we succeed in this project, and your drawings are actually published in the newspaper, what do you think they can offer that a written or photographic record cannot?

It has something to do with the tactility of the drawing and also with this 'liquefying of situation'. It's the special quality of the outline drawing that it is able to transform fixed things into action, into the fluidness of unfocused attention. Photographic recording is always contractive, in one fell swoop. By drawing I can release myself from these rapacious reflexes of perception. It is a form of recording that is both 'dissolved' and precise. There is a specific technique which has arisen over the years where I use the pencil like a pendulum. I'm able to produce drawings without preferential direction, avoiding any signs of a pretentious handwriting style.

Is that ever fully possible? Can you really grant full freedom of movement to the hand?

Everyone has a certain preferred direction from left to right, or from the centre, a basic movement. But I have found ways of avoiding those preferences with this technique, which developed by itself.

You are obviously trying to respond in a directly physical way to what is before you, but how do you achieve that state?

Each project goes through certain phases. I do not draw continuously and surrender myself to each location in an unpractised condition. Each location has its own idiom with all its preconceptions to work through in an initial period of extremely prolific drawing. Gradually the lines take over and my own authorship, my own will, takes a back seat. So I come into a certain 'flow' where I automatically succeed in recording a complex situation in its entirety, not in one fell swoop, but in a synchronous duration. This state lasts two or three weeks where I work the whole day through till I'm exhausted, and a kind of virtuosity appears.

You're completely absorbed?

Yes. When you're really inside a process, you disappear as an author. Then the line takes over and gets unbounded.

Question from the audience:

I have been thinking about this meditative state you get into, and wondering how much pressure it can be put under. You showed us a comic book one day by Joe Sacco while we were talking in your studio, which shows the Palestinian situation from a Palestinian perspective.[8] Do you think you could do the type of drawings you do in a situation where there was real human suffering, in a situation that was more fraught and dynamic and with all sorts of political issues?

I don't know. I do not seek extreme situations or sensations. But looking back, I have tried out various locations, from everyday ones to laboratories for pharmaceutical research with living animals... and there was also a coal mine, a slaughterhouse, a sausage factory. The slaughterhouse was no problem. In fact in all these places I managed to dissolve myself, after the initial problems, and to become a kind of seismographical instrument. But indeed I'm not a machine, and if the pressure became too much, I would cease. Our perception is determined by all functions of the whole body, also by its sentiments and its vulnerability. That is the main point, which should never be denied.

What determines your choice of location?

> Both intention and coincidence. One location often leads to the next one, just as the line flows from one point to another. Sometimes I am given commissions, and right now it makes sense for me to work on commissions, to be put in the same situations as photographers and film-makers.

Is it really much to do with coincidence? Surely it was your idea to go to the slaughterhouse.

> Yes, indeed it was, but it varies. Sometimes I also react to proposals or commissions, as was the case with the commission for the Albertina in Vienna. A few years ago I was asked to make an extensive portrait of the famous graphic collection there, and of the everyday life of the place and also of the construction work that was then underway. A film-maker was commissioned at the same time and on the same theme. In the end the director of the Albertina said he was astonished to find much more of the mood and of the very special atmosphere of this ancient place in the pure outlines of the drawing sequences.[9]

Why do you think it is that while some drawings describe a lot of what you're looking at, others leave off very early on in the process. One of the drawings made in Frankfurt Stock Exchange shows a man going upstairs, and there's nothing else, even the man is not

I don't judge the drawings while making them. Sometimes I start
to draw something, a dog maybe, which is sitting on the ground.
Suddenly he stands up and disappears. This break in time will remain
apparent when the sequence is assembled. Sometimes drawings
which seem to be unfinished become very important for the whole
sequence during the process of editing. As a quality of fleetingness.

I'm interested in the editing process. What are the guiding
principles, is it that you have a sense of a sequence of these images
that you want to arrive at, and then take out the ones that aren't
relevant, or is it that you are looking at a whole set of images and
making connections across the sequence?

I selected 482 drawings from those made here, and
discarded maybe 200. When doing that I have no
storyboard in mind as the director of a film or a
cartoonist does. Editing to me is an open process, there
is no fixed, rigid choice, no 'director's cut'. The selection
for a book, for example, is quite different than that for
an exhibition. A basic principle is to work out
connections present within single drawings and to
bring them into a fluid order. But there is no fixed place
for each single drawing. You can read the CS sequences
from different directions. They are not bound or
determined by a final intention, which incidentally, is
what makes most comic strips so boring. This is what
I am trying to indicate when I talk about the autonomy
of the particles: the unboundedness of the line in the
single drawing needs the unboundedness of the whole
context.

Kate Macfarlane was Exhibitions Organiser at Riverside Studios, 1985–89, and Director, 1989–90. Exhibitions curated during this time include 'Tim Rollins + K.O.S', 'Ilya Kabakov', 'Bethan Huws', 'Contemporary Art from Havana' and 'Louise Bourgeois'. In summer 2000, she co-founded The Drawing Room, a non-profit organisation devoted to the exploration of drawing within a contemporary context.

Notes by the artist and interviewer

1 'The Death of Life Drawing', Patricia Bickers, *Issues in Art & Education*, Wimbledon School of Art in association with Tate Gallery, 1996, pp 68–76.

2 'Duration' *(durée)*: a central term in the philosophy of Henri Bergson (1859–1941). It is a quality of time which is unmeasurable.

3 'Monad': a central term in the philosophical system of Wilhelm Leibniz (1646–1716).

4 Alexander Roob, *Theorie des Bildromans*, Rome/Cologne, 1997.

5 A.N. Whitehead, *Process and Reality*, 1929.

6 The initials CS are used to describe a specific form of sequential drawing, based on the shifting of perception. Like the process they describe, the meaning of CS has been subject to transformation over time. To begin with CS was an abbreviation for 'codex scarab', i.e. the loose sections of a codex which, in the manner of a scarab beetle, are constantly undergoing transformation. Other meanings of CS have included *colla sinistra* (Italian), usually an instruction for musicians, to use the left hand (or side of the brain); phonetically in German 'see it' (or 'look at it'); 'comic strip' or 'conservative shithead' (the latter a track by Napalm Death, a punk band).

7 Wilhelm Busch (1832–1908) was a German cartoonist and poet, who is regarded today as one of the main sources of the development of the modern comic strip. He also wrote a few fantastic short stories, among them *Eduards Traum*, about the journey of a Leibniz monad through the various dimensions. There are various editions of his complete works, and the Busch Museum is to be found in Hannover near the famous baroque park constructed by Wilhelm Leibnitz.

8 Joe Sacco, *Palestine – A Nation Occupied,* Seattle, 1996.

9 A.R., *CS VII – Albertina,* Klagenfurt, 1999.

In Alexander Roob's series *CS Protocol, Wimbledon School of Art*
there is no end of work: the work we see busy students engaged in;
the work represented by the hundreds of drawings themselves,
products of Roob's compulsive labour; the work demanded of us as
we interrogate what exactly we are looking at. We are perpetually
at the dawn of creation, and the slow accretion of a world being
formed has its rapid parallel in the lines with which Roob
constructs each drawing.

This method of representing all experience in outline leads to a
curious subtext within the drawings. As we witness students of
costume design and theatre technical arts measuring live models,
and from those measurements constructing clay models, the
strangeness of our need to model reality, to observe and diagram
the body, to create new bodies, becomes absurdly evident.

A student peers intently into the face he is creating. We begin to
realise that we too are peering intently, that we are experiencing
that student's attention, and moreover, Roob's attention as he drew
him. So we undergo this odd alternation: of first being drawn into
the rapt, synaptic exchange between artist-scientist and model; and
then of pulling back, to see in the candour of Roob's line one body
facing another body. We enter and then pan away from the obsessive
gaze, the obsessive drawing.

The drawings include not only what Roob sees, but record also
the act of perception in all its ambivalence, the oscillation between
acuity and stupor. Moments of beauty, humour and drama spark
and then disappear in the next frame, into the void of a drawing that
reveals nothing but an empty classroom, the nullity of a gaze.

These drawings are about the impurity of sight; the impossibility of
ever achieving a tacit, objective perception. The vertigo of perception,
the way we are always flailing for visual equilibrium, instituting

measurements and norms, is made explicit. Roob has selected the ideal form for his work. Drawing and perception are perfectly congruous in this sense: they are both impure, imprecise, and irreducible.

We seem to witness something being created, and witness its witnessing. The drawings, as simply constructed as they are, expand into three-dimensional space, where we find ourselves watching as Roob's line traces his perception. We are outside the drawings, creating them with the artist, but against him too, apart from him. We are inside ourselves, just on the cusp between what is perceived and what is recognised.

Seeming to 'simply' draw what he perceives as quickly as he perceives it, Roob spawns a universe of narrative. Or is anything really going on after all? To look at these drawings is to struggle between what we see and what we make of it.

Often the drawings allude to the world of the comic book; to pulp worlds of science fiction and horror, of boundaries transgressed, half-formed creatures cursing their makers, ancient evil reawakened. Roob's drawings possess an ultraviolet quality – they reveal other energies than those which are immediately apparent. His blunt, unobtrusive lines document the preternatural aspirations hidden beneath the unassuming toil of the theatre technical arts students: creation really is what goes on here.

Sometimes Roob's drawings suggest acts of Promethean creation, the backstage where the phenomenal world is prepared; or it is as if we have stumbled upon a band of adolescent elves, decked out in tank tops and baseball caps. At other times we can think only of torture and invasion. But no-one is being harmed.

One of the most ingenious of these spontaneous plot lines is the wry, clichéd theological game these drawings play: hosts of maker-gods hovering over their creations on one hand, and god as eye on the other. A graphic melodrama on the mercilessness of sight and the desecration concomitant with making. The will to harm that is twin impulse to the will to create. A gothic theology of the eye, of the maker.

And then there are individual drawings which are unexpectedly sensuous and strange, as in the drawing which consists of just a finger running along a pair of lips, either shaping those lips, or tracing the 'real' lips of a lover; and the viewer feels with intense immediacy Alexander Roob's own hand mimicking that movement on the page, his perception momentarily pre-empted by an eroticism that is both dreamlike and tactile. It is a collapse of moments, the touch of a sculptor to sculpture, pencil to paper, lover to loved; and finally the touch and weight of our own eyes.

At other times, there is a creepy sexuality, as figures buzz around a model like flies, brandishing callipers. If there seems at times to be an easy irony at work in the parade of students with their comical succession of callipers, cameras, chisels, pencils, it is the irony of self-identification. We (and Roob) are pursuing the same analytical trajectory as these students at one remove; we are equally complicit in the lechery of seeing, of recording.

In other drawings narrative empties out, and we have only the starkness of our own perception. The sense of story deserts us, in the drawing of drawings in particular. The drawer and his model are frozen in a kind of innocent stasis, a blank sheet of paper between them, teetering on the brink of representation. But instead of focusing on the equation unfolding between artist, model, and paper, we are swept by the next drawing into the swirling maelstrom of someone's hair, disoriented by a pair of feet floating in the air. When we should be attending, we are perceiving. When we should be perceiving, we are telling stories.

Often the eyes in Roob's work are ridiculously large, eyes as big as lemons. Eye seeks out eye, and we are drawn, just as Roob was drawn, to another perspective from which to look. If there can be said to be a protagonist, it is the eye. We see it in the sphinx-head facing off with a dumpster, pitting its affectless stare against the dumpster's own blankness. Or the huge glaring eye which protrudes from a head, propped on a pole, unseeing, defiant. The drawing in which a group of students are gathered, happily chatting, oblivious to the half-formed creature who has just opened her eyes behind them. Everywhere the concentration on the faces of the artists; you can't tell if these looks are those of apian industry or murderous absorption. The implicit glance of Roob himself, which could be either. Or neither, just a glance. Just a drawing.

And then ultimately, our own eye, the point at which our minds and the drawings converge. A pupil expands and contracts, a line expands and contracts. The drawings expand and contract in our minds like an eye.

Eric Ziegeweid

Eric Ziegeweid is an artist and writer. He graduated from MA: Fine Art: Drawing at Wimbledon School of Art in August 2001.

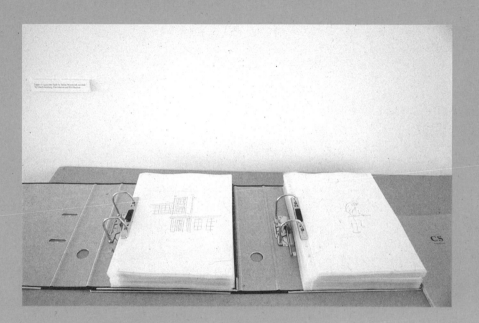

1 Robert Henri, 'An Address to the Students of the School of Design for Women, Philadelphia' (1901), in Margery A. Ryerson, ed., *The Art Spirit*, New York, J.B. Lippincott, 1958, p 80.

2 On the contingency of drawing and its epistemological reach, see Erika Naginski, 'Drawing at the Crossroads', *Representations*, no. 72, Fall 2000, pp 64–81.

Given the avant-garde's long-standing investment in non-traditional media, alternative spaces of exhibition, and unorthodox modes of expression, something as venerable as the practice of drawing runs the risk of being overlooked if not entirely dismissed. One can easily imagine finding the contemporary artist in wholehearted agreement with the American painter Robert Henri who, in 1901, assessed drawing as time less than well spent: 'Oh! Those long and dreary years of learning to draw! How can a student after the drudgery of it, look at a man or an antique statue with any other emotion than a plumbob estimate of how many lengths of head he has.'[1] The study of the nude, the disciplining of vision, the lessons of the academy: if drawing still bears the stamp of an inauspicious past, it presumably does so at the expense of its own visibility and vitality. Yet it is difficult to deny that the visibility and vitality have a long and complex history. From doodles to diagrams, from Neoclassical outline to Surrealist automatism, from Raphael's blind stylus work to Henry Moore's notebooks: these are expressive arenas that each in their own fashion bear witness to the kinetic charge of *disegno* – and to an imaginative process that signals not, in fact, an archaic and passive mimicking but an active and tactile operation that pairs gesture with concept only to bind material and metaphysics together, and to force subjectivity and objectivity to collide in very peculiar ways.[2] Drawing thus continually asserts its self-sufficiency – as the Romantic valorisation of the sketch made clear in the first half of the nineteenth century – and that its substance can lie in something other than those tired mythologies of secrecy and sacred genius to which the preparatory stages of artistic production tend to fall prey.

To dismiss drawing as a conventionalised pedagogical tool offers little insight into its relevance beyond the predictable role it can play as the fountainhead of a cultural scholasticism of the most retrograde sort. But the logic of that dismissal may sound familiar to readers of modernism's champions. A comparable scepticism was

3 Clement Greenberg, 'The New
Sculpture', *Art and Culture*, Boston,
Beacon Press, 1965, p 140.

marshalled against sculpture, for instance, first by the French
poet Charles Baudelaire in his *Salon of 1846* then a century later by
the New York School's advocate, the art critic Clement Greenberg.
For Greenberg especially, sculpture's 'handicaps' (as he called
them) were self-evident; an age-old association with the monolith
and a slavish commitment through modelling to anthropomorphic
representation were the root causes of its sterility. Sculpture was,
in sum, '*too* literal' – its medium ill equipped to do anything but
studiously reiterate the animate world. It had yet to relinquish the
aesthetic values to which Leonardo da Vinci's *Vitruvian Man* had
given free rein. Greenberg might have said the same of drawing.
And this would not have been because sculpture and drawing
are actually alike (although it is safe to say that Henri's account
of drawing antique statues – which highlights a mutually shared
academic allegiance to the human form – suggests just this
possibility). Rather, the pronouncement would have resulted
from Greenberg's belief that both were somehow not up to par
with painting and the accomplishments its means of expression
afforded.

Or at least not yet. This was the state of affairs between 1948 and
1958 when, in an expectant frame of mind, Greenberg contemplated
the terms of sculpture's rebirth. Was it possible for sculpture to
relinquish three-dimensional humanistic illusionism in order to do
what abstract and nearly abstract painting had done, that is, 'deal
with all imaginable visual entities and relations' by exploring 'the
greatest possible tension between that which was imitated and
the medium that did the imitating'?[3] The answer seemed straight-
forward: sculpture should relinquish the nobility of terracotta,
marble, and bronze for the mass-produced look of industrial steel,
glass, and celluloid; it should instil a constructivist spirit in its
practitioners by cutting, casting, polychroming, and assembling
things together; it should, in other words, put the lessons of Cubist
painting and collage to good use.

To stress that the canon of modernist painting – from Claude Monet to Jackson Pollock, Georges Braque to Helen Frankenthaler – occupies a privileged place in Greenberg's *paragone* is to rehearse a well-known truism. The thesis of its primacy rests on the capacity of medium to assert the purity of things such as its own concreteness, literality, and immediacy. But what interests me about Greenberg's dilemma in the fifties is less the familiar terminology of formalist modernism (the teleology of flatness as it applies to painting) than the idea that an artistic practice – an artistic practice like, say, that of drawing, which currently struggles against accusations of imminent obsoleteness – needs to assert as well as to test the limits of its autonomy in order to ensure that its lyricism and vividness continue to make themselves felt. Lyricism and vividness, I imagine, are a good part of the reason why a progressive institution such as Wimbledon School of Art could find, in the six-week residencies its Centre for Drawing makes possible for working artists, something akin to a laboratory for aesthetic play, discussion, discovery and display. Indeed it is remarkable to think that the Centre is the first of its kind in the United Kingdom. So how might we establish new grounds for drawing's *raison d'être* in today's artistic situation? Are new grounds in fact necessary? Yes and no, as the works produced by the Centre's first three artists-in-residence suggest.

We can explore why this might be so by considering how some of those works put into relief what Michael Ginsborg has called, in the introduction to this publication, drawing's 'closely defined set of conditions': monochromatic flatness, the linear network as opposed to the colour relation, and the wilful trace pencil, ink, charcoal or chalk leave on the piece of paper that inevitably functions as its support. This is drawing's economy of means. This is the material foundation of its autonomy – the essential mediumness, as it were, that Robert Rauschenberg famously had the cheek to subvert, in 1953, in the *Erased de Kooning Drawing* all the while leaving the original image's ghostly imprint, its Benjaminian aura, there for the viewer nostalgically to ponder. It is also, by the same token, the essential mediumness that Ansuya Blom elegantly problematises in the *House of the invertebrates* series that was the outcome of her residency. Blom's approach along these lines is wittily complex. The support for drawing here is not the ominous tabula rasa offered up by the sheet's white expanse. Blom begins with something altogether different: snapshots taken while 'visiting a site in New York'. The architectural realm of institutional interiors is then hauntingly recorded on ink-jet prints made from photographic negatives whose blue-grey hue dramatises their wraithlike feel. The Albertian perspectival box, in other words, serves as preface to the drawing phase only to find its rigorously ordered spatial effect competing against an abstract, calligraphic trace deploying itself in a floating, ectomorphic skein of white gouache. As Blom's title for the series intimates, then, the body as animate presence is neither anthropomorphised nor the sublime, architectonic measure of its surroundings. Drawing becomes instead a literally disembodied medium, as though its autonomy had been subjected to an x-ray machine only to leave line dangling as a negative of itself – a meandering skeletal scaffolding without structural integrity, a white transcendent event taking place over the dark ground of representation.

At first glance, Alexander Roob's series of 482 images entitled *CS – Protocol: Wimbledon School of Art* seems rather more prescriptively attuned to drawing's 'closely defined set of conditions' than Blom's project ever could be. An economy of means is strictly enforced by Roob: pencil, white paper (the small sheets each measure 15 by 21 cm), and an even-handed outline that records on page after page the unfolding of an art school's daily routines. Where subject matter is concerned, Roob's insistence on the objective nature of his task purposefully rejects the aesthetic stance implicit in the redolently subjective secrecy in which drawing can often find refuge – a useful

4 Theodor Adorno, *Aesthetic Theory*
(1970), trans. C. Lenhardt, London
and New York, Routledge & Kegan
Paul, 1986, p 243.

reminder that while 'subjectivity is a necessary condition of the
work of art,' as Theodor Adorno put it, 'it is not by itself an
aesthetic quality.'[4] Indeed if the artist-cum-reporter here is for the
most part studio-bound, he is acting as a peripatetic witness to the
public theatre of his subject. That theatre, we discover, gets played
out in the guise of a kind of formal and material irreducibility that
is not unlike an updated version of John Flaxman's drastically
simplified treatment of line. Furthermore a radical economy of
means does not instigate a quelling of expressive potentiality (in
either case). For the notion of visually serialising what really takes
place in an art school – the teaching and learning of the nuts and
bolts of making that underlie the pygmalionesque endeavour –
yields anything but a temporally coherent narration of the creative
act. Roob repeatedly draws students working directly from the nude
model under scrutiny – gauging, sawing, groping, and manipulating
the marionettes of their own making – and an intensely clinical,
scopic, and sexualized image of violence unleashed on the
simulacrum is the end result. One of the more startling aspects of
watching Roob's roving eye and hand is the revelation that life
drawing (drawing from life) is a deeply disjunctive and shocking
undertaking and hence anything but outdated.

Vong Phaophanit too finds the deliberate limiting of means to be,
paradoxically enough, altogether liberating. He renounces the
illustrative, technical, hidden, and secondary status drawing for the
most part maintains in his practice. And he allows paper, ink, and 'a
little bit of pencil' to be self-sufficient and to initiate the quiet
sounds of making. Much of the eloquence of marks and traces, then,
is the subtle cacophony of 'scratching or pushing or rubbing or...'
that lingers in their margins. The autonomy of drawing accordingly
shifts its terms to privilege a proto-surrealist 'experi-ence of the
unconscious: the empty page' as well as to provide the battlefield
for the trace's encounter with the sign. On the latter point
Phaophanit is adamant, and this situates his works on paper as part

5 Amédée Ozenfant, *Foundations
of Modern Art* (1928), trans. John
Rodker, New York, Dover, 1952,
p 249.
6 Adorno, *op. cit.*, p 349.

of a long-standing modernist tradition that carefully peruses the
contingent relation between mimesis and semiosis. One finds echo
of his stance in Amédée Ozenfant's *Foundations of Modern Art*, for
instance, where one of the central claims is that 'the language of the
visual arts is made up of categorical forms, which are only signs, as
it were, inadvertently.'[5] Nowhere is this more impressively
conveyed than in works like *as a raven* or *as a fish* in which titles
and ink forms – a figure of speech and a visual morphology, two
essentially unlike things – are conjoined, the comparison offering
the viewer the spectacle of simile in action.

What the new drawing does, to conclude, is simultaneously to define
and transgress the boundaries of its physical and formal autonomy.
This reflexive and analytical capacity is perhaps not entirely foreign
to the terrain of aesthetic thinking. But it is, I think, a most
powerful instantiation of what Adorno once eloquently called art's
'polemical self-consciousness'.[6] Polemical self-consciousness, that is
to say, prompts drawing to proclaim the unquestionable authority of
its medium (however that medium might be construed). Polemical
self-consciousness likewise gives drawing the crucial room it needs
to find a productive place for itself despite a climate that is not
always so welcoming – and it is to that place that each of these
artists contributes in a different way.

Erika Naginski

Erika Naginski teaches art history in the History, Theory,
and Criticism Section of the Department of Architecture,
Massachusetts Institute of Technology. She is currently
a junior fellow at the Society of Fellows, Harvard
University.

Acknowledgements
We are extremely grateful to
everyone who contributed to the
Centre for Drawing's first year:
Ansuya Blom, Vong Phaophanit,
Alexander Roob; contributors to
this publication: Guy Brett, Ian Hunt,
Kate Macfarlane, Erika Naginski,
Claire Oboussier, Eric Ziegeweid;
outside speakers for a programme of
lectures relating to the residencies
and exhibitions: Penelope Curtis,
Head of Henry Moore Institute
Programmes, Siân Frances, court-
room illustrator, Vivien Lovell,
Director of Modus Operandi, David
Maclagan, artist, art therapist and
lecturer at the Centre for
Psychotherapeutic Studies,
University of Sheffield, Simon
Morrissey, curator and writer,
Angela Weight, Keeper of Art at the
Imperial War Museum; staff and
students at Wimbledon School of Art,
and in particular Peter Armsworth,
Jean Austen, Elaine Banham, Naran
Barfield, George Blacklock, Frank
Brown, Rod Bugg, David Burrows,
Miranda Clarke, Marilyn Cutbill,
John Dunn, Erno Enkenberg, William
Furlong, Katie Gibson, Katherine
Ginsborg, Julie Hancox, Dereck
Harris, Christine Hatt, Angela
Hodgson, Tim Johnson, Rebecca
Fortnum, Phil Machon, Nick Manser,
Robert Mason, Rebecca McLynn,
Kim Merrington, Melissa McQuillan,
John Mitchell, Piers Nicholls,
Colin Painter (previous Principal),
Michael Pope, Rosie Potter, Elizabeth
Rosser, Allan Sly, Keir Smith, Jennet
Thomas, Allan Walker and Stefan
Woodward.

The Centre for Drawing at
Wimbledon School of Art was
established in October 2000. It is an
experimental gallery project that
aims to promote and re-examine
contemporary drawing practice.
Currently being run as a pilot, the
Centre for Drawing hosts a drawing
residency once a term in a dedicated
space at the School, followed
immediately by an exhibition of
works produced. This publication has
been produced as a record of the
Centre for Drawing's first year.

In future, documentation of the
Centre for Drawing will feature in an
annual refereed journal. Potential
contributors are invited to submit
proposals.

The Centre for Drawing is a
Wimbledon School of Art Research
Centre project.

The public conversations with the
artists were held as part of the
'Agendas, Agendas, Agendas' series of
events organised by the Research
Centre at Wimbledon School of Art.

A version of Angela Kingston's essay
appeared in Issue 10 of *Engage*
magazine which focused on drawing
and is available from Cornerhouse
Publications.